Contents

This project supported by Cooperative Agreement No. 97-CH-VX-K001 from the Office of Juvenile Justice & Delinquency Prevention, Office of Justice Programs, U.S. Department of Justice. Points of view or opinions in this document are those of the author and do not necessarily represent the official position or policies of the U.S. Department of Justice.

OJJDP Office of Juvenile Justice
and Delinquency Prevention
Office of Justice Programs ◆ U.S. Department of Justice

Poem by Danielle, age 10,
who resides in family foster care.

Who Am I?

There was once a tree full of apples
Which was my family.

Then one day I fell off.

Some grown-ups came and put me in a pear tree.

Then I fell off.

A little boy came and put me in a
tree with apples, oranges, pears, and peaches.

Then I fell off.

Then I sat there forever wondering
who will pick me up next.

Where will I go? Will I go where I belong?

Or will I waste my life living with
fruits who I don't belong with because they can't
encourage me to accomplish my dreams, or can't
tell me who I am
because they don't know who I am.

It's up to you.

Who am I?

Foreword Anna Quindlen

All writers have their regrets: a poorly wrought phrase here, an unconvincing character there. Paging through my scrapbooks and notebooks from decades as a reporter and a columnist, my regrets are both less tangible and more real. Rising from the scribbled notes and the yellowed clippings are the children, children beaten and bruised, neglected and abandoned, ignored or unloved. Sometimes I met them at schools, sometimes in foster homes or in government offices. Occasionally I reconstructed the story of their lives while they themselves lay in the city morgue.

It's impossible to be a journalist and retain any passion about the work without thinking that it does some good—to open the doors and windows and let daylight in. But it's also impossible to be a human being and walk away after a story is over and not feel as though you've abandoned the people and chosen the prose instead. This is doubly true when the story is the story of a child. More than doubly true. A hundred times. A thousand.

This book recounts a different kind of story, the story of the people who decided to become, not journalistic observers, not horrified onlookers, but engaged participants. As one couple who tells their story here admits, "Our daughter said she was tired of listening to us complain about how sad the news always was in the paper and on TV—how nobody helped make a difference. It was our time to either put up or shut up."

This is the story of the men, women, and children of CASA, an acronym familiar to judges, lawyers, and families across America. The Court Appointed Special Advocates program was begun 25 years ago by a judge in Seattle who felt he needed more information about the children whose futures he was deciding in court. The CASA program trains ordinary people, working people and retired people, men and women, college educated and simply street smart, to become advocates for kids, to learn all they can about an individual child and his individual troubles and struggles, and to report back to a judge about what the child needs as fairly and clearly as possible. It may be a kid in foster care whose birthparents want him back in their home. It may be a kid with disabilities whose mother is fighting for extra help in the classroom. It may be a group of kids, brothers and sisters, who have been driven apart by the legal system and who need to live together again. There are as many different kinds of cases as there are CASA volunteers.

The program is growing in leaps and bounds, so that any number written here will certainly be out-of-date by the time you read this. But by the end of the year 2001 alone, there were more than 50,000 ordinary people working as court appointed special advocates. It is no exaggeration to say that they are the human component in a system that too often seems like a misery machine. The lawyers know the statutes, the social workers the regulations. But the CASA volunteer is assigned to know the child, one child at a time, to understand the boundaries of her life, to telephone her teachers, to consider her hopes and dreams, to try to come to some conclusion about what will be in her best interests. For children whose pasts have been chaotic and whose futures are uncertain, the CASA volunteer may be the most consistent, interested presence in their lives.

Sometimes the most important job of those volunteers is to inject common sense into the situations they encounter. Dick Milton, who received CASA's Advocate of the Year award in 2000, has made it his business to try to reunite siblings who have been parceled out to different foster homes, operating under the logical assumption that their brothers and sisters are all the family many kids have left. Beverly Tuttle, an advocate from South Dakota, discovered that the Native American teenaged sisters she was assigned had been placed in a juvenile detention facility for cutting school—to care for their quadriplegic mother. This CASA volunteer set out to find someone to care for the girls on the reservation until their mother could care for herself and for them. In one case in California, a teenager who had been in a foster home for many years was diagnosed with cancer. State policy required that she be placed in a special facility, so at the moment she was facing terminal illness, she was also facing the loss of the family she had come to love. It took Jan Miller, a CASA volunteer, to find out that the foster mother could get a waiver, and that the sick girl could be returned to the only real home she had ever known.

Sometimes small and simple solutions can make the difference between misery and contentment. But with so many children who are sexually, physically, and psychologically abused, CASA volunteers find themselves dumbstruck by the depth of suffering they encounter and saddened by how little they can do. "The right recommendation isn't always clear," says one. "Sometimes it's the lesser of two evils, but you are the one who has gotten all the facts to make that recommendation."

Many volunteers know that they have had a hand in keeping a child with a mother who is far from first-rate; many have watched as children were placed for adoption, even though they had living parents who professed to want them.

This is not a process of "happily ever after," although there is some of that. But it is about being certain that the interests of the child are clearly understood and articulated, even when there are no easy answers. It is about visiting homes in which you are not welcome, and going to schools in which teachers have given up hope. It is about meeting children who recoil from a hug because they have never had one before. So how can it be that it is also about

deep satisfaction and commitment, about people who say they have become their best selves while trying to help one child toward a good life? Perhaps, like most of the work the CASA volunteers do, it is the small moment that tells the story. A volunteer from Florida named Brenda Gowan ran into one of her former kids, a boy named Paul, at a park. It was several years after Brenda had been involved in the case in which Paul was taken away from his mother after he was sexually abused by his mother's violent boyfriend. Brenda was on another case at the park when Paul ran up, jumped into her arms, and whispered, "I remember you."

"How are you doing?" Brenda said.

"See these pants?" the boy replied. "They're brand new. They cost $25 and they're mine."

Just that. Just pants. They're mine.

I dare you to read this book without weeping.

I dare you to read this book without anger.

I dare you to read this book without thinking about becoming a CASA volunteer.

Brenda Gowan, Tarpon Springs, Florida

It all started for me when a friend of ours, who was a judge, brought a CASA volunteer to church to share information about the program. I'm not really good at shutting up about things that matter, so as my friend, the judge, was walking out after the talk, she tapped me on the shoulder and said, "You know, you could really do this. Be a CASA volunteer."

That gave me a lot of confidence, so I decided to go ahead and give it a try. I thought about how everybody always says they want to make a difference. That's the way people measure their success: I am successful because I made a difference in the world. But as a CASA volunteer, you make twice as much of a difference—you feel better about yourself, but more importantly, you make a difference in the life of a child. I just didn't see how anybody could say no to that.

So I said, "Yes, sign me up for the training." Of course, you don't really know what you are getting yourself into until you actually experience it. Sometimes it's really simple—you pick up your file,

I'm not really good at shutting up. I'm not going to sit there in court and not say anything. Not when I can make a difference.

1

review it, and then you go do whatever that child needs, and everything runs just like they said in the training classes: 1, 2, 3, 4, and you're done. And sometimes it's not easy at all. It depends on the child. It depends on the case. But I talk to parents, teachers, doctors, psychiatrists, psychologists, neighbors, sometimes even the utility company if I think it will help. It just depends on what I need to know.

One time I encountered a criminal judge who had just been rotated onto the family law bench. But this judge didn't want to be there and didn't know what a CASA volunteer was. So there I am, the little volunteer with the CASA pro bono attorney sitting next to me. And I'm asking for additional time to submit my report because the father is in Indiana and the mother's in Florida, and I need more time before I can make the right recommendation. Then this judge made a comment that if we had people who were paid for doing this job, we wouldn't have to give them additional time. I was greatly insulted by that, ready to crawl across the table and tell him that there's no way he could afford to pay me for what I did. But I didn't. I held on. And he gave me more time, so I got what I needed.

But that incident was the exception. Most of the time the judges are very open, welcoming the CASA volunteer's input and opinions. And I have positive proof that judges listen to us. I was in court on behalf of a 6-year-old girl named Joanne who had been sexually abused by her mother's boyfriend. So we were in court, and the mother had her own attorney and the father had his attorney. I don't remember why they had separate attorneys, but somehow they had managed to get them. The Department of Health and Human Services was there with their attorney. And I was there by myself, because this was only a five-minute status review, and CASA couldn't spare a pro bono attorney for what I could handle on my own.

So the judge talked to the mom's attorney and got all this input, talked to the dad's attorney to get input, and the Department's attorney. And then the judge turned to me and asked me, as a CASA volunteer, whether I had anything I wanted to say. Well, I would never pass that up. As I explained, I'm not really good at shutting up. I'm never going to sit there and not say something. So I just said, "Well, Your Honor, I just want to make sure you know that this little girl, Joanne, is ready to be adopted. And we're just sitting here waiting. We're ready."

And all the attorneys were laughing at what I had said. Here was this dumb CASA volunteer who didn't seem to know that we hadn't even started the termination of parental rights. But the judge looked at me (he was very, very cordial, very nice) and he said, "Well, Mrs. Gowan, there are certain things that we have to do, and we just have to take the time to do them." I said, "Okay." But six months later, we were all in court again for the pre-trial conference to terminate parental rights so that Joanne could finally be adopted and be safe. All the attorneys were there again, and this time I had the program attorney and my case coordinator with me. And this time the judge turned right to me and said, "CASA guardian, if I remember correctly, you are in favor of this and you are ready to go." And I thought, "Yes!" I mean, the attorneys had laughed at me before. I didn't care. Go ahead, let me look dumb. The judge knew what I was waiting for, he knew where I stood, and he remembered that.

To me, that shows the phenomenal influence a CASA volunteer has. We don't have to be attorneys, and we don't have to be psychologists and psychiatrists, and we don't have to have all of the etiquette.

We can go in there and say what we have to say, and because we are volunteers, sometimes our political incorrectness is okay. We still get our point across.

The CASA volunteer has a totally different view than everybody else. And only the CASA volunteer really knows what the child needs, sometimes more than even the mother or father, because of course the parents are self-serving. They are worried about how it's going to affect them, what the outcome says about them as a parent or something, not always thinking what's in the best interests of the child. And the Department of Health and Human Services has statutes it has to go by that may not always be in the child's best interests either. So even though CASA volunteers have to accept legal parameters, we still know the child and what he or she needs better than anybody.

That's why we are doing all this in the first place—to help the children, to make things better for them. While all my cases are memorable, I remember my first case the most because I was a little bit scared and more easily intimidated back then. There were three children: Ryan, 4; Natalie, 5; and Jason, 6. All of them were developmentally delayed, neglected and abandoned by their parents. They didn't know how to identify colors, how to count. The 4-year-old, Ryan, wasn't even potty trained. I had never been in a situation where I met a 6-year-old child who couldn't point to a picture of a dog and tell you that it was a dog. These beautiful children , they didn't even know how to hug. You'd pick them up and hug them, and they would arch back and move back away from you, but not because they didn't like you. They just didn't know what you were doing to them. So I remember going to Jason's school, watching him sit in a corner all by himself. Of course, he was in special classes because he had never been around other children and didn't know what to do. So I walked over, and I sat down next to him and tried to get him to look at me, but he wouldn't look up. So I said to him, "My eyes are brown. What color are your eyes? Maybe we have the same color eyes." And of course, he didn't know what brown was. So he looked up to see what was wrong with my eyes! And I think that, for me, was the most memorable thing, because I immediately thought, "My goodness, I can do something here. I got this child to look up. I got this child to smile."

So of course I remember those children, especially Natalie because she really had a hard time. She wouldn't hug, wouldn't look, wouldn't talk, wouldn't do anything except throw Spaghettios™! So I kept trying to look for any positive change in her now that all three children were living with their grandparents. One day I went over there. I'm a hugger whether they like it or not. I hugged Natalie, and for the first time she actually put her arms around my neck, and I thought, "Ooh, we've got something here; we've made progress." She didn't exactly know how she was supposed to do this, to hug, but she knew that it was a good thing and that she liked it and she was looking for it. And it just made me feel really good that I was able to work the system for them.

I remember when it was time for Ryan to go to a special school; I made sure he got a school backpack. He kept walking around in the house, asking, "Is this mine?"

"Yes, it's yours."

And he walked around for a few more minutes, and then he came back and asked, "Is this just mine?"

"Yes, it's yours."

"Do I have to share?"

"No, you don't have to share."

"Okay. Is this mine?"

"Yes, Ryan, it's yours."

"Okay, can I sleep with it?"

"Yes, you can sleep with it."

That night I imagined that little boy asleep with his backpack on, and that was fine with me. So that case had a really good ending, because the three kids are now safely living with a grandmother and grandfather who love them, who send them to school and make sure that they are healthy and growing.

It's hard for me to speak about only one case. As I said, all of the kids are memorable. There was another time I was a CASA volunteer for this little boy, Paul, who was a victim of sexual abuse by his mother's boyfriend. He was in foster care when I first met him. He had been so severely abused sexually that he wouldn't even talk. Now I don't feel comfortable with the children telling me about sexual abuse because I'm not a psychologist or psychiatrist, and I want to make sure I don't say the wrong thing. I don't know what to do with the information that I have, so when I hear about sexual abuse, I try to make sure that I guide the conversation to a different area and then get the children to counseling as soon as possible with professionals who can do the most good for them. So Paul was involved in sexual abuse counseling and was doing much better. And I'm talking to the counselor: "Do I need to know anything before we go to court? What can you tell me?" Turns out that the one who abused the boy was a skinhead.

So now I needed to go visit the skinhead. After a little work, I located the place where he was living—I wouldn't call it a house—but I found the place. He gave me very bad directions, but I found it. So I went up and knocked on the door, and he didn't answer it. I drove my car down the street and pulled up under a tree and waited for him to come back. And he did. I said, "I need to talk to you. I'm the CASA volunteer for your girlfriend's son."

Well, you know they always like to impress you, and I guess he thought he was impressing me by inviting me in, telling me what a safe environment this would be to bring the child back into. So as I was taking notes on this, I'm looking past his face to the wall. And there's something all over the wall. I couldn't figure out what it was, but it bothered me because it was red and crusty-looking, not like a normal food stain. I concluded my interview and left, still not knowing what was on the wall, which drove me nuts. Luckily, my husband happens to be a CASA volunteer, too. So two days later, I set up an appointment to meet with the mother at the boyfriend's house. I told my husband, "I'm going to sit, take the interview, and you go see if you can figure out what's on the wall." Well, when we got there, of course, this time they knew I was coming. They had cleaned the house up, had put the chair in front of the wall to hide the stain. So I'm sitting there taking notes, while my husband tries very casually, without looking like he's investigating anything, to find out what's on the wall. The mother wanted to know what my husband was doing. And I said, "We are just trying to see why there is ketchup on the wall." The mother just looked at me, and said, "That's not ketchup—it's blood." They had gotten into a fight, and the skinhead had fired a gunshot at the mother. That only confirmed in fact what we knew instinctively—that Paul couldn't stay there. It's hard for me to keep calm when I hear a person has hurt a child.

I want that person prosecuted, and I'll do whatever I have to do to get what I need, as long as it's moral and legal. Bad people don't intimidate me, and they don't scare me, because I figure anybody who hurts a child is not much of a person anyway.

After all that, the mom still said she wouldn't terminate her parental rights. So we figured we would have to take her to court. But while Paul was in counseling, the therapist asked him to draw a picture of the person who hurt him. Well, when you're a skinhead and you've got a swastika tattooed on your forehead, it's pretty easy to identify you. I got the psychologist to write a letter and attach the picture. I put it with my CASA report, sent it to the court, and before we even got to the courtroom, mom signed the surrender. Because how can you argue with that? Your own son drawing a picture of the person who abused him.

So you do make a difference. After a case is over, CASA rules say we aren't supposed to have contact with the kids—just let them get on with their lives. But once when I was at a visitation for another case at a park, I saw Paul. Maybe it was two, three years later. Anyway, now he was in an adoptive placement,

and he was doing very well. But our rules say don't make contact. So I turned and walked away so he wouldn't see me, but I was still observing the visitation with the other case I was working on, and all of a sudden Paul came running up to me, jumped in my arms, and whispered in my ears, "I remember you."

I said, "You do?"

He goes, "Yes, I remember you." And it just gave me cold chills. Obviously, I was a positive memory for him, or he wouldn't have jumped up in my arms and hugged me. So I put him down, and I said, "How are you doing?

He said, "See these pants?"

I said, "Yes."

He said, "They're brand new. They cost $25 and they're mine." I loved it. They cost $25 and they're mine.

So you make a difference, not only in the kids' lives, but also your own—even my daughter's. Before CASA, I had never been much of a volunteer person, and I think I wasn't setting a very good example for her. Once she saw me get involved and what a difference it made, she wanted to do the same thing when she was old enough. And in her senior year in high school, she did some volunteer filing for the CASA program.

Like I said, I'm not really good at shutting up, so here's the real thing I want to say: If you get your yellow pad, your map, your pencil, and you head down a one-lane dirt road to a house with three cars, four dogs in the yard, and weeds up to the window and know that you're at the correct address, you might be a CASA volunteer. If you knock on the door and hear the television playing and the pitter-patter of feet running away, you might be a CASA volunteer. If you pound on the door because you know the people you've come to visit are home and you call out through that shut door, "Hello, I'm not going away until I check on the children," you might be a CASA volunteer. If you enter the house and sit talking to the mom. If the baby in the highchair eats his spaghetti with his hands and says good-bye by smearing his ketchupy hands all over your new white pants, you might be a CASA volunteer. If you work many hours finishing your report to the court, pushing for a better situation for a child, all the while saying, "I will never take another case," you're probably a CASA volunteer. If the next week, when the phone rings and the case coordinator says there's this child in trouble and we need you to take another case and you say yes, you probably are a CASA volunteer. If you get out your little yellow notepad and your map and your pen, and pull out your old jeans and head down another little dirt road, you, my friend, are definitely a CASA volunteer. And you must continue to fight the good fight because without you, these children, who are our future, will never get out of the house on the little one-lane dirt road.

Rick Neyrey, Houston, Texas

I have always been a materialistic sort of person. I could just never get enough of things. I would buy a used car, and a year later it's like I wanted the same car, but now I wanted it new. I'd go through corporate America, where I'd been taught to never be satisfied with the status quo. Always push for more, push for more. And it was getting to where I was not feeling satisfied with receiving, with getting, because I always wanted more. Through some internal process, it dawned on me that I could become satisfied by giving. So I was in my mid-30s and at the point where I was looking to find a way to start giving back. One day, I was driving down the freeway when I heard a radio advertisement about CASA. To be honest, there was nothing unforgettable or memorable about the words in the ad, other than the idea of helping abused children. But it was the hook that I needed to hear. Because my wife is a licensed social worker and deals with domestic violence cases on a daily basis, I guess I'm sensitized toward working with abused kids. When I called the local chapter, I learned that CASA needed a lot more male

It's like giving presents to children who are waking up with the magic in their eyes at Christmas. Seeing that pure joy on their faces when they get that gift they'd just been dreaming about. I see that on the children I deal with in CASA.

volunteers, especially as the older boys tend to respond better to men. So I went to the CASA orientation and the training. That was three years ago.

One of the cases I'm working on now concerns an 8-year-old girl named Briana, who was removed from her home environment due to neglect when her mother and her mother's boyfriend were arrested for felony drug charges. The three of them had been traveling in a motor home when the adults were busted by the Houston Police for 50 pounds of marijuana and an ounce of methamphetamine. The boyfriend had resisted arrest, punched an officer in the face, while the mother tried to release an attack dog on the rest of them. So when I first got involved, they had already been on the run for more than a year using aliases. Briana had not been in school. That's the environment she came from.

I met her the first time at the foster home—a very pudgy 8-year-old girl, curled up in a ball on the couch, sucking her thumb. Her beautiful red hair hung down over her face. When I initially sat down to talk to her, there was absolutely no verbal response. When I left the foster home an hour later, not only had she started talking with me, but as I got up to leave, she jumped up, threw her arms around me, and said, "No, don't go. I want you to stay. I want you to stay." And she said, "Promise me you'll come back tomorrow."

I said that I couldn't come back tomorrow, but that I would come back on the next weekend. Would that be okay? And she said that would be great. That was my first encounter with Briana.

Since then, the case has unfolded more and more. As I said, the mother was arrested for felony drug charges. While I had been getting to know Briana, we discovered that the U.S. Marshall's office in West Virginia had outstanding warrants on the mother's boyfriend. The boyfriend was a fugitive convict, with an arrest record that was two pages long. Real colorful character. From evidence the police discovered in the motor home, we learned the boyfriend was not only an active member of the Ku Klux Klan, but was also past president of the Pagan Outlaw Motorcycle Gang, a group defined as a criminal gang by the FBI.

One of my first priorities was to get the child some counseling until I could get her out of foster care and placed with an appropriate relative. Early on, Briana hinted about things that occurred while they were on the road. She talked about the mother doing drugs. She said she even tried some of them herself but got sick, so she threw them away. Right before she left foster care, she started hinting about inappropriate sexual conduct with the adults, the mother and the boyfriend—talking about how she would watch them have sex, how she had been sent to fetch a vibrator, things of that nature. The therapist reviewed a series of issues with Briana, and about two months later, the child revealed that she had had

sexual contact with the boyfriend while the mother was present; that in fact, the mother had wanted to join in. Once Briana was able to get these secrets out, let go of her burden, she was more able to engage and her therapy really took off.

Meanwhile, I was investigating other family members to find the right placement for Briana. I located

a relative in Florida I thought might be suitable, but when Children's Protective Services conducted a home study, it was only a page long, with no checked references. I challenged the home study in court and pushed for more details. I interviewed the family members myself and dug up more extensive information, which resulted in placing the child with the appropriate relatives about 60 days later.

To show just how much a stable home environment can do for a child, when Briana was first taken into custody at age 8, she could not count change, tell time, or even do basic math. Six months later, after being placed with caring relatives and attending school regularly, she's making good grades, mainly A's and B's. She recently told her therapist that she has never been this happy before.

"I do not want to go back and live the way I used to live. I do not want to go back to my mom."

What does this all mean for me? Well, obviously it's very satisfying. State social workers work very, very hard, but they only have so much time they can devote to any one case. And I know that the demands of this particular case definitely surpassed what time CPS could dedicate. If I, if CASA, had not been involved, chances are this child would have been in foster care much longer, would not have gotten into therapy, possibly would not even have gotten to the point where she could disclose the sexual allegations in enough time so that we could make appropriate recommendations to get her the additional services she needed and ensure the court understood what was going on. She might also have been returned to the mother!

Sometimes when I talk to my friends about what I do at CASA, their first reaction is that it must be very depressing since so many horrendous things happen to the children.

"How can you do that?" they ask me. "You must have trouble sleeping at night."

And my response to them has been that I sleep much better at night knowing that there are people like me, other volunteers, working for organizations like CASA, who are making sure this doesn't happen again to this particular child. And I sleep much better at night because of the difference this organization makes. It's not disturbing to me to know what's going on. What's disturbing to me is thinking that it would continue to go on or even escalate if I wasn't involved. Because of CASA, an 8-year-old girl no longer has to live her life on the run, using aliases, having to carry a firearm, being told that police are murderers, being told not to trust anyone outside of her family. I helped change a child's life—not so much me as an individual, but me as part of an organization. I think the best way to look at it is that it's sort of like Christmas morning, giving presents to children who are waking up with magic in their eyes. Watching the pure joy on their faces when they get that gift that they'd just been dreaming about. I see that in the children I deal with in CASA. When I walk into a room, they light up. It's like magic. It makes the hair on the back of my neck stand up. I can go to bed that night not wanting any more—completely satiated. No object, no shiny new car, no raise in salary, has ever left me so fulfilled.

Julie Hobson, Granville, Ohio

I live in a small town, a college town that is pretty well-to-do, and I come from a fairly privileged upper-middle-class background, so in a way I guess it is unusual that I am devoting this part of my life to working with disadvantaged children. My work with CASA came about secondarily. I'm currently working on my dissertation for a Ph.D. at the University of Pennsylvania, studying reading and writing literacy among students who hail from poorer backgrounds.

Working at home on my dissertation, I thought it would be good to get myself out into the world by volunteering for a few hours each week. Mainly, I was looking to do something that built on what I'd already done. I've volunteered in schools, I've done three Junior Leagues, and I've done hospital benefits and edited cookbooks—all things that were useful, but they didn't really impact people's lives the way I wanted to.

Then I read a magazine article about an abused child who was returned by the courts to his parents'

> *I've volunteered in schools, done three Junior Leagues, and worked hospital benefits, but nothing impacts people's lives the way CASA does.*

home, only to be abused again and eventually killed. In the article, the judge was quoted as saying that if he'd had more facts about the case, he probably wouldn't have returned the child to his family. The article went on to talk about CASA and how it was founded to do exactly that: provide family law courts with as many facts and details about a child's situation as possible and serve as that child's advocate so the facts wouldn't get ignored.

After I read the article, I went online to the national CASA website to find out more. Now that I've become involved in cases myself, I understand why the CASA program needs to be so thorough, but initially I was surprised by how extensive the volunteer screening process was. You had to write an essay and participate in a long interview, but I found it really interesting because the CASA coordinator helped you explore your own childhood and discuss your expectations in terms of being a volunteer. Many of the volunteers I met in the trainings thought they would become like a big brother or a big sister to the child, but we quickly learned that CASA is not about taking the kids to McDonald's for a hamburger.

You're really a gatherer of information, which you then organize and present. Hopefully, you build an argument. At the end, you go to the judge, to the court, and say, "Here's my best recommendation in the best interests of this child." And the right recommendation isn't always clear; sometimes it's the lesser of two evils, but you are the one who has gotten all the facts to make that recommendation. I've been a volunteer for two-and-a-half years, and so far, the judges have given me everything I've asked for, which gives me a lot of confidence. Sometimes you recommend exactly what the state does. Actually, my experience with Children's Protective Services is that they are pretty much on top of things.

Still, I can do what they can't. I document every phone call, every visit I've made, the people I've talked to. I triangulate, as they say in my field. I don't just take one person's word for it—I go and double and triple check the information. It's not enough to just listen to that little voice on the phone saying that everything at home is fine. I call the school and make sure the child is attending school and find out how he's doing in school. I see his report cards and talk to his teacher. Over the years,

I've talked to learning disability teachers, psychiatrists or psychologists, health care workers, grandmothers, grandfathers, and foster parents. In most instances, by the time you get the case, the child has already been removed to foster care for safety reasons. You start to get a pretty clear picture of the type of world in which the child operates.

The author E.M. Forster wrote in *Howard's End* that the only important thing in life is to connect with another person. I think for me that's what volunteering is about, connecting in some way with the lives of these children. And their former families. And their new families. A number of the children have been adopted into foster families and moved away to California, so I don't have contact with them anymore, but I still feel connected to their futures in some way. And I'm connecting also by learning about a world that I've not been familiar with.

One of my cases centers around a little boy, Dave, who's been in foster care for more than four years. He originally was removed from his home because of neglect. It wasn't a physically abusive home, but he was found hungry, with a swollen stomach, he and his three siblings. They had no food in the house. The toilets were clogged with human waste. The bathtub was full of cold, dirty water. An eviction notice was sitting on the table, and the mom had left. She was simply gone. A neighbor found the children naked in the front yard. So I went over to see Dave, who was covered with mosquito bites. He was severely troubled, psychologically disturbed. He'd caught a bird and killed it. He's tried to set his house on fire three times. He jumped in front of a car about four months ago. Last month he tried to drown himself. He threatened to kill his mother. He tried to kill one of his brothers. But right now he is with a foster family, who as far as I'm concerned has a special place in heaven. Dave will, if I have anything to say about it, never go home. He does not want to go back to his mother, whom we eventually located living in her car. We tried to get her to go into counseling with him, but she shows up maybe once a month out of the four sessions, and nothing is working. It's as if the mother and the child are playing off two different sheets of music, and they will never be playing in the same orchestra. The psychologist is going to court with us next week to say that Dave should not be returned, that he should stay permanently with this foster family. My guess is it's going to be difficult to find an adoptive family who will take a child this troubled, and even though the foster family will keep him until he is eighteen, they are not interested in adopting him themselves.

But I still feel we've made progress in a lot of ways. Dave knows me pretty well. He told me the other day that he wants to marry me when he grows up. And that if it weren't for me, he would be going back home to his mother. He is a beautiful child, but no one has ever taught him the difference between right and wrong, good or bad. When he does things, he shows no remorse. He also can be very outgoing, loving, and just an amazingly nice, terrific kid. He sometimes gives me presents to take to his little brother. He'll draw pictures for me. He'll come and bring a book, and we'll go through it. He'll sit on my lap. He'll touch and hold my hand. He can be a very expressive child.

One time I took Dave and his brother out to dinner, which isn't normally something a CASA volunteer does, but it was the only opportunity I could find to see him and his brother outside their foster home. So I took them to a cafeteria. When they were younger, Dave went without food for so long that now he kept going back for more plates, even though he hadn't even eaten the food he had. Pretty soon the table was covered with plates. I said, "Dave, you have to stop and eat." And he just couldn't. He had to keep going back for more. And he still hoards food. His foster mother said he still worries about food all the time. He told me about being a baby and crawling to the refrigerator and trying to find some food, when he was still crawling. He has vivid memories of being very, very hungry. At any rate, if I'm there to serve as his advocate, he's a child who won't be going home. CPS has filed twice to return him home, and we've gone back in and said no. This mother doesn't understand him. She's told me she will whip him and hit him until he behaves. So this is how I feel I make a difference, even with such a sad case. Dave is already on his sixth caseworker. They keep switching them all the time. So I am a consistent person in his life who keeps the threads going.

It's always one of those questions—who benefits here? In CASA, I think it works both ways. You have the chance to see a child's life really changed for the better. At least I've noticed that, and the volunteers I've talked to say it happens all the time. So from my

experience, I guess I've benefited by becoming more tolerant. I think I didn't realize how hard it was to live on welfare, or not on welfare, because a number of the families I'm involved with in Ohio are almost at the end of their welfare benefits now. I guess I thought it was easier than it is to survive down in the depths of where some of them are—coming off drug addiction and abusive husbands and coming out of jail trying to get jobs. They live in neighborhoods where they're robbed. Landlords don't make the necessary repairs. At one of the houses I visited, the door was held shut with a box. All of the food was on the counter because there were rats. And they contend all the time with problems of daily living, consumed with just getting through what, for me, is easy. Just doing laundry involves going many, many blocks away. Their cars break down. They get sick and they can't afford medical care. Life is tough.

And I can help them with a lot of these issues. I get on the phone to the caseworkers and request bus vouchers so a mother can get to the women's clinic. Whatever it's going to take for a mother to function better with her child, in her home, getting her house ready for the child to come home to, is to me one of

my jobs. I've been on the phone with Section 8 Housing to make sure they get adequate housing. I've talked to their CPS social worker about how we work on budgeting. I even help them with basic skills like cooking.

One case I was working on, the mother called to ask me how to cook a chicken. Somebody had given her a chicken at a food pantry, and she had no idea how to cook it. She had never done it before. Her own mother had died when she was 3, so she had no role model, no reference point for being a good parent. I've come to understand that the mothers don't know how a mother is supposed to behave. So they need those services like CPS. And they need what I do. They need lots and lots of support systems to help them learn what I just take for granted. What was somehow imparted through my family, they don't have. They're usually pretty isolated. Although they have some relatives around, nobody can help them much. They're all busy working two and three shifts on other jobs, as well as dealing with problems in their own families. Being a CASA volunteer has broadened my tolerance for how hard it is for these families to get their lives together. I've learned a lot from that. And I'm far more understanding when I read a news story or I see something on television about how hard many of these people's lives truly are. It's not so much about class as much as it is about economics.

In general, my CASA work has sort of validated my life experience up to now. I am a mother, I have had jobs, and I can share some of those background experiences with the people I'm working with, so I can relate to them on that level.

To do this job well, I think you need to be organized and disciplined. And you need to be able to ask questions and keep confidences. But mostly, I would say if you'd like to do a volunteer activity that allows you to connect with the life of a child, and maybe more than one child depending on the family, in what has been for me the most meaningful volunteer activity I've done, I think you ought to look into CASA. It doesn't take a lot of time, and you get to apply what you've learned over the course of your life to improve the life of someone else.

Achaessa James, Seattle, Washington

Some people get involved with volunteer work for strictly altruistic purposes. Me, I was motivated by anger. I was angry about how, in many ways, I was robbed of my own Indian heritage. But more angry at watching Native American kids suffer from the effects of drug and alcohol abuse at home and then suffer some more from a legal system that doesn't really know anything about Native American cultures or communities.

Even though he knew his blood father well, my father was raised on the reservation by a non-Native American family, and they made him feel so ashamed of who he was and where he came from that, until I was 30 years old, I never even knew who his blood family was. And my mother's family acted the same. Even though we would often have Indian uncles coming into the house to dry out from too much drinking, my mother's family would always say, "Yeah, they're Indian, but you're not."

They didn't say it to be mean—they were from Oklahoma, and life had taught them to never admit

It's you and the kid and the court system, and the judges want to hear what we CASAs have to say. We're the ones that paint the picture of the child for the judge. The social worker will come in and list a string of symptoms and a string of causes and a string of services. And the attorneys will come in and represent their positions. But we come in and talk about the kids. We talk about the family.

you were Indian, or else your kids would be taken away to boarding school or some other place, and you would never see them again. However, I wound up being sent away from my mother anyway. When I was 9 years old, my mother was arrested one night for drunk driving. So of course I got sent to a foster home when they took her to jail. I spent a number of scattered years between birth and age 17 being raised by my sisters, both of whom were many years older than me, and already married with families of their own. Between being passed around a lot and hearing contradictory things about my heritage, I just never knew where I fit in.

So kids have always been important to me, especially protecting kids from the effects of drug and alcohol abuse. Before I became a CASA volunteer, I had done a lot of volunteer work over a number of years, and I always wondered what kind of results my work really had. I mean, you can do fundraising and you can do mailings, but you really don't always know the results of your work. Even serving on a nonprofit board does not have the same kind of direct impact on the people whom you really want to help.

The work I did with Indian kids before CASA was outside the judicial system, and it was way too affected by community politics. It was always very frustrating to be working on an endeavor and then watch the project erode because of personality conflicts or different community policies. Working with CASA is very exciting for me, because community politics are not in the picture at all. It's you and the kid and the court system, and the judges are very open to what we CASA volunteers have to say. The judges know we're really the only people out there who have direct contact with the children in a non-clinical way. We're the ones who paint the picture of the child for the judge. The social worker will come in and list a string of symptoms and a string of causes and a string of services. And the attorneys will come in and represent their positions. But we come in and we talk about the kids. We talk about the family. We make this a real situation to the judges, so they know they are getting a human perspective, but the judges also know they are getting an unbiased and intelligent perspective.

One particular case sticks out for me that involved three young sisters: Katy, Megan and

Jenny. When I first took the case, the girls were 3, 5, and 7 years old respectively. Their mother was a drug addict living on the streets, so the sisters had been in a couple of different placements with relatives. But when the last sober caregiver died, the sisters were placed together in a foster home outside the city. And I need to say here that I represent urban Indian kids, who are very different from the Indian children who are connected with their reservation. Generally the family is scattered all over, some on the reservation, some in the urban areas. It is very difficult to find extended family members, particularly extended family members who are stable and healthy.

The only placement that could be found for these three girls together was a non-Native American woman in Eastern Washington. The woman emphasized that she had been married to a Native American man for 20 years and their kids were pow-wow dancers, but the husband was no longer in the picture, and he wasn't from the same tribe as the little girls. Both the social worker and I had some concerns because the children were entirely removed from their specific tribal culture. Non-Native

American folks think "Indian" and picture a generic culture, but it's not like that at all—this woman's children were from a coastal plateau tribe and the girls are from two plains tribes, and these are distinctly different traditions. Well, I recommended we do it anyway, because it was the only way we could keep the girls together. The foster mother seemed to genuinely love the kids, and she was very open to the girls having periodic visits with their grandmother and one of their aunts, provided that the relatives only visited when they were sober. So things went on that way for about two years. The mother remained an addict, and the grandmother and aunt continued with their own alcohol problems, so we were moving toward termination of parental rights, which is always a very, very serious step to take. But the foster mother really loved the girls, really wanted them, so we began the process of negotiating an open adoption.

But then, a red flag went up for me. The foster mother had in the past said she was open to having the girls' relatives come visit and spend time with the girls. But when we got down to the terms of the actual agreement, she suddenly changed her mind and said she wanted to restrict visits to once a year. That concerned me a lot because the girls had a really close connection with their grandmother. I told the social worker about my concerns before leaving on an extended trip.

When I returned a month later, I learned that the girls' mother had died of a heroin overdose. Obviously, the grandmother wanted to have the girls at the funeral. She also asked if the social worker could help her track down her son, who had been adopted years earlier, to see if he could come to his sister's funeral. (This was the first time I had heard that the girls had an uncle, and the girls' case record had no mention of this family member.) So the social worker tracked down the son, and it turned out that he had been adopted by extended family members who were clean, sober, and healthy. They all showed up for the funeral, and the girls were comfortable with them right from the start. And then it turned out that the brother of that adoptive mother—he and his wife—were in the process of getting licensed to be a foster family because they wanted to adopt a kid. So after we ran all of the genealogy charts, we discovered that they were distantly related to these three girls on both the mother's and the father's side, and they were very interested in bringing the girls back into the family. We thought this was a great thing, especially since they resided in the Seattle area, living near the grandmother and aunt. So this was where it got very complicated.

Should we go ahead and allow the non-Native American foster mother, with whom the girls were very bonded and had been residing for two years, to adopt them, knowing they would be raised apart from their specific tribal culture and their blood family? Or should we place the girls with members of their extended family, members of their own tribe, whom the girls didn't know but who lived nearby and were blood kin, even though they had only recently thought about being foster parents?

These are never easy decisions, and my role as a CASA volunteer was to talk to all the parties involved, especially the girls, and recommend what I believed was in the best interests of the children. So of course when I spoke with the foster mother about the new chain of events, she was very unhappy and disappointed. She wanted the children. The adoption agency wanted her to have the children. But the

Department of Social and Human Services (DSHS) and I wanted to slow the process down a bit, just until we could make sure we had all the facts. Four days later, the foster mother petitioned to take the girls out of state, to take them to Mexico for a vacation the following week. My initial instinct was to say no, fearing that she would take them out of the country and we would never see her and the girls again. First, I asked her if she'd be willing to postpone the vacation for two weeks to allow the girls a couple of visitations with their new-found relatives. The foster mom said definitely not—even though it was a driving vacation without plane tickets to cancel. That strong reaction worried me even more, and I spoke with the social worker about my fear. She agreed with me and wanted to deny the petition. But I knew it was important that the social worker maintain a good relationship with the foster mother and the adoption agency since she would need to work with them again. So I told her that I would play the "bad guy" and say no. I took the heat for that decision, and my instincts turned out to be right in a way, because when the foster mother was told no, she simply drove the girls to the DSHS office that afternoon and abandoned them there. Fortunately, the other family was ready and willing to take the girls. So now these girls have been with their extended family for nearly two years, and we're in the process of finalizing their adoption.

In their new home, they are quite active in school. Megan is taking karate lessons, and they're all developing in ways that people never imagined. The two youngest, Katy and Megan, are affected by Fetal Alcohol Syndrome, and Jenny, the eldest, has always been very protective toward them. But now that they have stable adult figures in their lives, Jenny has become more of a kid again, knowing that she now has real parents, a mom and dad who love her and her sisters. The coolest thing of all is that now the children get to see their uncle and other relatives all the time. They hang out with their cousins. They take vacations to their reservation. I mean, really, they are more involved in their family now than they ever have been—and even more than they

could have been with their birth mom. The grandmother is now sober and remarried to her ex-husband. The whole family has really blossomed since the mother's death—a sort of wake-up call to them all, and it's very exciting to watch. While I know that the children I work with are in better shape than they would have been had they stayed in their previous situations, I consider this case my best success because the kids not only got to stay within their family, but the whole family has healed itself and is functioning as a family again, not just disparate parts. That's especially challenging for urban Indians, because we all got sent here from places all over the country. There are different tribes that would never have met, would never have come together, and there isn't ever "one group of my own people in my own place" type of thing. And so, to be able to bring a family back to itself so that it functions as a unit greatly excites me.

To me, this is the most fulfilling part of my job. I mean, granted, I love going to court, and I love being able to state my case and know I'm being heard, but really, the most deeply satisfying part is helping people learn how to be a family again. I can be sort of an intermediary in helping them understand and learn how to communicate, because in dysfunctional families that's the problem. Nobody talks. Nobody knows how to communicate without upsetting somebody. And everybody's afraid of or angry at the "system." So in that regard, I'm sort of a mentor. Maybe that means so much to me because of my own childhood, but all I know is that now I have found a good use for my anger.

Being a CASA volunteer has literally changed my life. Strangely, after all the things I went through as a child, feeling betrayed by my family and by the courts, I actually ended up going to law school. After I joined CASA, I decided to take two years off from my career and devoted the majority of one of those years to doing my CASA work. Some of the cases were really heavy and involved, and they needed my attention. Few CASA volunteers ever do that, but I was in a place in my life where I could. Not that I had a lot of money—I was living pretty much hand-to-mouth. But the work was so important, and it clearly needed to be done. At that point, I literally was the only person available to do it. I still get angry or outraged sometimes at the injustice or the craziness of the people involved in the system. And I worry that we don't have enough CASA volunteers, especially to serve the Indian community. In King County where I live, in 1999 there were more than 600 Native American kids in the court system who needed a child advocate. Only 300 of them had a CASA volunteer assigned, and of those CASA volunteers representing those 300 children, only five of us were Native American. This is why we need Native American CASA volunteers. Of course, there are lots of good-intentioned, non-Native American volunteers who want to help, and their efforts are greatly needed, but Indian families in crisis (just like anyone in crisis) feel more comfortable opening up to a person who they know comes from a cultural background similar to their own. Indian folks have enough of a tragic history to know to be scared of outsiders, even when we know those people just want to help. It's sort of like the difference between having a bad cut or scrape and going to the doctor or going to your mom. You know the doctor will take care of you, but you're kind of scared of anyway. But when you go to your mom or your grandma, she puts on the bandage, and then she opens her arms and you sit on her lap and you go to sleep. They both treat the wound, but with family you feel safe, secure. That's what I do. That's what CASA does.

Kathleen Simmons, Liberty, Indiana

I have such a tremendous desire to help these children because I was once one of them. When I was 5 years old, my mother started to beat me— literally would stomp on me, kick me because I would not be submissive. I wasn't alone; I had five brothers and sisters. None of them graduated from high school; one is in prison in Texas on two counts of capital murder. Who knows where the others are, probably trying to survive any way they can.

James, the oldest, was never abused, and he was held up to a higher standard. Louis and Bernard would go along with the fighting to keep our mother from really hurting them. John was hurt a lot. He was a weird kind of kid, who would rather play pretend baseball with his fingers than anything else. Then there was "the princess"—Christina. She did whatever my mother wanted her to with guys, so she was not beaten on a regular basis. And there was me.

Childhood was a very dark time for me, but there were many people who showed kindness here and there, making a world of difference in the long run—

Being a foster child isn't in your blood. No child is destined to be without a family.

people who made it possible for me to survive. I remember in the seventh grade, it was a cold, snowy day in Edinburgh, Indiana. I was on the playground, no gloves, no hat, no coat, wearing a boy's sweater that had been handed down to me and a pair of ratty jeans. I was very hungry and very, very weak. I kept passing out, and the other kids were standing around laughing and making fun of me. Then my teacher, Mr. Van Wye—he was a great teacher—picked me up out of the snow and carried me into the school building. He took me into the guidance office and called the nurse. They tried to reach my mother, and of course they couldn't reach her. They finally got ahold of my uncle, my mother's biological half-brother. He and his wife came to school and got me. They questioned me about what I'd had to eat. During the course of the entire weekend, I had eaten half a honey bun and shared a 6-ounce Coke. In three days' time that's all I had had to eat.

So they took me to their house and they put me into bed and gave me some chicken noodle soup. I actually ate chicken noodle soup out of a can for the first time in my life that day. I felt so privileged! I was living that day. I also got some crackers and a nice nap, and then my biological mother showed up.

I was terrified because I knew if she got her hands on me, she would probably kill me. My uncle tried to keep my mother out of the house, keep her at bay, while I grabbed my books and things and ran out the back door. I knew I had to make it home before she did. Of course, when she showed up, she kicked me, she slapped me, she hit me all over. It was terrible. And then she left with some guys in a car. My uncle found a police officer, and the two of them went to this judge's house. The judge wasn't even at work — he was on vacation. And without proper documentation or anything, they pled my case to this judge. The judge then told my uncle to go with the police officer and get me. If it was really that bad, they were to go and get me right then. As the judge, he would go out on a limb, and he'd deal with the paperwork tomorrow.

After that, I lived in several foster homes. The biggest thing I remember was that there was no one to talk to. I didn't have a sounding board. Nobody asked me how I felt. Everybody made assumptions about me, treating me like I was a number and they were just punching the clock for the day. But it was my life we were talking about! In foster homes where there weren't any other children, I was treated more like a "gofor," you know—a live-in maid service. Sometimes I was treated like an adult who had already grown up. And in foster homes where there were other children, I was always set apart in a negative way from the biological children. They'd make comments like, "Oh well, we expect D's and F's from her," (even though I didn't get them). They'd say, "She's below normal. It's in her blood." Being a foster child isn't in your blood. No child is destined to be without a family. And even though I was angry and frustrated, I knew there was a better life out there for me.

So, you see, I have a connection to these kids. I know what they're going through, literally. And I can provide them hope. Helping children has become a way of life for me. I work at Union County High School as the study hall monitor. I'm affectionately called "The Warden." I also work at the Juvenile Intake Center, where they bring the kids in after they've been arrested. The kids in this community see me a lot in many different places.

And on top of that, I'm a single working mother. I have this motto: just because I have two kids of my own doesn't mean I can't help others. If there's a kid out there who doesn't have a home, as long as I have one, that kid has one. I'm kind of the safe house. I will pick up kids who are in trouble at a moment's notice and give them a bed to sleep in, a nice safe haven for however long it takes to get them back into their house or into a foster home somewhere or a group home.

Becoming a CASA volunteer was a natural extension for me. When I was going through my divorce, the lawyer who I worked with found out I had been a foster kid. He was also the County Attorney for all the kids in this county, so he started talking to me about CASA. I intrigued him because I had been in foster care and could really relate to these children. He just kept on me about it, and every time he saw me he would ask if I was interested. And so I went to an introduction class and became a CASA soon after.

I'm just getting assigned to my first case right now, but there are lots of kids I already know in this county who are being served by CASA. Kids come up to me all the time at school and ask me to talk with them. They ask me how to handle situations, what to do if their mom's hitting them, and different things like this. And of course, I abide by the law and report everything, but I help them too. I try to help give them some ideas on how to diffuse the arguments.

There's this one particular young girl at school, Alicia, who is extremely loud. She opens her mouth, and you can hear her at the other end of the building. She just really has a set of pipes on her. And she's very troubled. Always draws attention to herself, gets into trouble. Nothing too severe, but she gets into quite a bit of mischief. So the first day at school as a freshman, Alicia was yelling and carrying on in the hallway. And so I called her name. And she looked at me and I looked at her and I said, "That is no way to behave."

And she said, "But why?"

I said, "Because you're a young lady."

"No I'm not; I'm a girl."

I said, "No, you're better than just a girl — you're a young lady. I see that in you, and sooner or later you'll see that in you." And she just looked at me; she was so shocked. Well, about an hour later she was in my classroom, and when she realized it was me, she went, "Oh no." And I looked at her and smiled and said, "Oh yes." But she has become closer to me because I give her guidelines and boundaries, and I also give her praise.

It all comes down to compassion, giving someone a chance. When I was very young, I had tuberculosis. And a man, who remains anonymous to this day, paid for me to take an experimental drug because I was allergic to the tuberculosis medicine, INH, which is most commonly given. This man didn't know me. He lived in an entirely different county. But he helped me. He paid to have groceries delivered to my home. He paid the school to send tutors over so that I wouldn't miss out on an entire year of school. I don't know his name; I just know that he was compassionate. So how can I repay the countless people who did all these positive things in my life? I can't. There's not enough money in this world for me to pay them back. But I can show how thankful I am by giving to another child, extending that same opportunity. And hopefully, that child then will turn around and bestow the same courtesy to another. Until we get the chain going.

Sebastian Stubbs, Sr., Macon, Georgia

Macon, Georgia, is a peaceful, slow kind of town—a place you want to retire. So for some people it may be hard to imagine that there are kids living there going through very, very tough times. But they do, which is why they need me and others like me through the CASA program. Some of these kids have been raped, beaten—all types of abuse. But when you break it down, pain is pain. And a lot of times, they are meeting people in suits and ties, and these kids know that these people really don't care about them. But when they meet me and I explain to them what I do, that I represent them in court, that I speak for them, it sort of changes things.

One young man I met was 16 and needed spinal surgery, but didn't want to have it. I told him about my own difficult back surgery, how hard it was at first. When I opened up to him, he started to see that I really did care, that I wasn't getting paid for this and came here on my own free time. He started to trust me, and we talked, got to be good friends. And I expressed to him how important it was for him to get the surgery.

Kids just need to see more black men out here in the community, see them every day in their neighborhood, walking up and down the street, doing positive things, not selling drugs or hitting women or abusing other children or themselves. If they see more positive men helping in the community, doing something without being paid for it or looking for anything in return, I think that no matter what color they are, it will start to change the way that kids look at people, and the way that they start to look at themselves.

It's important to be real with these kids, show them they're not alone. Because I've been through pain, I know what it's like to hurt on the inside; the kind of pain people can't see, because they only see your face. I can relate to these kids; I understand exactly what they are going through.

My first CASA assignment was to assist Pete, who was just 6 months old when I met him. Pete was a child who had to have a daily shot to help his blood flow. If he didn't get his shot, he could die. And he had a young mother. I think she was either 16 or 17 at the time. The baby came into the system because his mother kept moving constantly from apartment to apartment, so medical services wasn't able to find the family to give Pete his shots. So the medical people called Children's Protective Services (CPS), and the case was initiated at that point.

Pete was in intensive care when I first met him, and he was so little you could practically hold him in the palm of your hand. He had all these tubes coming out of him, and he looked so pitiful—more tubes than infant. He had tubes in his feet and his hands and his stomach, and he'd had several operations because he would just stop breathing at a heartbeat. So his chest had been opened several times. Here was this tiny thing, lying sick in a hospital with no mother. I was new to CASA still, so I was kind of scared. I didn't really know what I was doing myself. But once I got in his hospital room and introduced myself to the nurse, she said that I could hold him. So I held him, sat down in the rocking chair in his room, and we rocked, and by the time I put him down, four hours had passed. From that point on, I knew this was what I was supposed to do with my life.

I think that's why I became a CASA volunteer. God put me and that child together for a reason. The CASA director could have given that case to anybody, but I think in some strange way, God had a hand in assigning this child to me. From that day on, that child became very special to me. He's like my son. In other words, I've gone beyond just being a CASA volunteer for him. I'm his "BoBo Daddy." And that makes me feel so proud, to think that he thinks of me that way. He has a way when he's real comfortable with you—he will rub the back of your arm, which he's done ever since he was 6 months old. He'll just kind of rub you, and I guess that's his comfort zone, like a pacifier or something. And whenever I hold him, he'll get the back of my arm and rub it.

I've watched him grow from 6 months up through 3 years old now, and I've been there for every birthday party. When he was put back into the system, he went into what we call a "granny house," a sort of group foster care home. I was there every other day. I think the people thought that I was spying on them rather than coming to see Pete.

But then something great happened. I asked his 72-year-old great-grandmother whether she would be willing to raise him. I asked her, even though I knew that her husband had just had a heart attack and needed care of his own. But she and her husband had raised 22 children of their own, and I knew if anybody could help this child, it would be them. Pete just wouldn't eat. He had to have a tube put in him to eat. The great-grandmother thought about it for all of a minute, then quit her job so that she could be with Pete full-time. And lo and behold, when he was put into her custody, given her love, he started to eat.

And once he was up to a certain level, the doctor said, "Well, I think I need to take out part of his liver

to make him eat more," and both his great-grandparents and I thought that was a real bad idea. We fought against the doctor, and we got the courts to allow us to send Pete to a specialist in Atlanta. The doctor there said, "We're not going to operate on him. If he eats, fine, but if not, we'll find some other way." We took the tube out, and the child has been eating ever since. And he's growing up. He's about 25 pounds now, and if you see him, he's just pure sunshine.

He's 3 now, about to be 4 years old, and he can count and everything. And here's a child who they said would not talk, would not walk, would not do anything, and if he did do those things, that he would be so far behind the other kids that he would almost be in a retarded-like state. Today, I would put him up against any 3-year-old in the country. He can say his ABCs, he can count, and he can sit down and hold a conversation with you.

And I'm glad I was here to help because CPS at first didn't want Pete to be placed with his great-grandma. Because of her age and the circumstances surrounding her husband with his heart problems and because of Pete's health, they were kind of thinking, "Well, maybe this couple is too old." And the last thing I wanted was for Children's Protective Services to put this child up for adoption. Because anybody who saw him wanted him. He kind of has

that effect on you—once you see him, well you just feel that you can't let him get away. So in order to keep him in the family, I needed to find somebody who could care for him, and once I sat down with the social worker and explained the situation to her, she overlooked the age factor when we came back to court. I expressed my concerns to the judge, and he agreed that there was no other place better for that child than to be with his great-grandmother.

I think there is a particular need for men to be CASA volunteers because, with the young children that I've seen and had a chance to work with, when it comes to discipline, a lot of times the boys don't pay attention to the young women working at the group homes. When I went there, I asserted myself to let them know that I was there to help them—I wouldn't be disrespected. They would stop doing a lot of the bad things that they were doing, and sometimes they even said to each other, "Mr. Stubbs is going to be here soon, and I'm going to tell him what you did."

So I think men need to be out in the front, pressing this thing because kids need discipline. I think men can bring discipline, not that women can't do it, but I think if kids see more men doing more positive things, then that will make a big difference—because there's nothing like a man trying to teach a young boy how to be a man.

Probably 87% of the kids that we see in the juvenile court here are kids of color. And a lot of times these kids, they have $100 sneakers, $150 sweat suits, and things like that because they want whatever they see on television or videos. But nine times out of ten, these kids are never going to see that kind of lifestyle that's on TV. So if kids could see more black men out here in the community, if they could see them every day in their neighborhood, walking up and down the street, and if they could see these men doing more positive things, rather than selling drugs or hitting women or abusing other children or themselves, if they could see more positive men helping in the community, doing something without paying for it or looking for anything in return, well, I think that's what our kids need to see, whatever color they are. They need to see more men doing things unselfishly. And I think once these kids start to see that there is a reward in helping other people, not just looking for something for themselves, I think that it will start to change the way that kids look at people and the way that they start to look at themselves.

Susan Forstadt and Stephen Forstadt
Los Angeles, California

We wanted to get involved with something where we could work directly with children, more hands-on than fundraising. Our daughter said she was tired of listening to us complain about how sad the news always was in the paper and on TV—how nobody helped make a difference. It was our time to either put up or shut up. That's how she put it, and of course it was exactly the push we needed to get started. So she helped us to do some research over the Internet, and we learned about CASA and how the organization helped changed children's lives as they made their way through the legal system. When it comes to abused or neglected children, what courts decide are probably the most important decisions for those children's lives.

Usually, the children that we work with don't have anyone to stand up for them or to fight for them, not only in the court system, but in educational matters, in medical matters, in family matters. We just go ahead and do whatever a loving parent would do for a child to get the services the child needs.

These children that we deal with have been dumped. They've been dumped by parents. They've been dumped by relatives. They've been abused. They've been abandoned. It gets to a point where they don't trust anyone. A CASA volunteer tries to renew that trust, and we succeed in many cases. And when a CASA volunteer makes a promise, a CASA volunteer keeps a promise. This is something these kids are not used to.

All too often judges have to make decisions without knowing much about the children, or in many cases, the information they have is inaccurate. That's where a CASA volunteer comes in. A CASA volunteer provides information to the court so that it can make an intelligent decision. A CASA volunteer is an advocate in court and an advocate for the child in everyday life. All it takes for us to do what we do is a willingness to help out and some common sense. That's all that's required.

One case we had concerned two brothers, Steven and Thomas. Steven was known for acting up and bad behavior. At the same time, he would hardly speak. It wasn't until he got placed in a foster home with a very loving couple that we learned he had a hearing problem. It turned out that hearing aids in both ears ended up correcting a lot of Steven's frustration and his bad behavior. Actually, it was an amazing case all around. This foster family wanted to adopt both boys, which seemed fine with the courts, though of course you have to go through a long process to make sure the children will be okay by talking with all parties involved. As we dug further into the case, we became aware that there was

yet a third brother, a younger brother, Brian, in a different foster home that nobody in the system seemed to be aware of. Steven and Thomas were very young, so they didn't remember Brian either. Once we found Brian, the couple who wanted to adopt Steven and Thomas took Brian in and said, "We'll take him too." As for Steven's hearing problem? Well, after he was adopted and started receiving proper services, we arranged to meet the boys at a bowling alley to see how they were doing. All three of them came running up to us, and Steven kept talking and talking and talking. He just wanted to tell us everything that had happened since the last time we had seen him. The hearing aids, all the help he was getting, enabled him to come out of his shell, and the adoptive parents were joking and saying, "We created a monster—now we can't shut him up." It's a good feeling when you see a child go from one extreme to another and the affection that not only you have for them, but the affection that they show to you, almost as if you're part of the family. We're real proud of that case.

There was another case, though, that wasn't as easy. We had been working on this case for nearly

four years. It involved a child who, by the age of 6, had already been placed in 13 different foster homes. Just about anything bad that could happen to a child had happened to Derrick—mental abuse, physical abuse, and sexual abuse. Now he was in foster home number 14, and it just didn't seem to us to be a safe place, based on our visits and talks with Children and Family Services.

Fortunately, we were able to get Derrick removed from the home, and we found a woman, a foster mother, who was willing to take him in. Derrick was almost impossible to take care of. Because of what Derrick had been through before he was 6, he was very, very difficult to handle, with many severe emotional problems, as well as medical problems. But this foster mother stuck by him, and we learned yesterday that adoption proceedings have been finally approved. We've been working very closely supporting this woman for about four years now, and the change in Derrick today is absolutely amazing. He'll always have problems, but he's so much closer to what we would call a "normal child," that it's just amazing to see what a loving home can do for children who have never had anything like that in their lives. So it's a nice story because it's not very often where we see the end result come out so well.

Another story we remember concerned a mentally disturbed boy, Michael, who was very withdrawn and was in, for a lack of better words, a "facility" because Children and Family Services couldn't find a placement for him. They were ready to put him in a mental hospital, diagnosed as prepsychotic. We had been to court with him maybe a dozen times before, and whenever we went, we would take him to lunch to help make it a little easier for him. But one time when we went to court and asked the judge for permission to take him to lunch, one of the attorneys got up to object, saying he had information that Michael was going to run away and that it wasn't safe for us to take him out because he would disappear. The judge asked if we had any response to that. All of a sudden, Michael jumped up, and he yelled out to the judge, "Run away—where am I going to run? No one wants me!"

The judge looked at us and said, "Mr. and Mrs. Forstadt, would you like to take him to lunch? Wherever you would like to take him, be my guest."

That is one of the best examples of how CASA volunteers get support from the court. In the case involving the young boy who had been in 13 placements, there were lots of complications, and the judge really, really worked with our information. She frequently set court dates closer together so things could be monitored more closely in the beginning, just so there was a check and a double check on the child. In fact, when we were getting close to the point of finalizing the adoption, the adoptive parents asked if the adoption could take place in this particular judge's courtroom because she seemed to take such a keen interest in the boy.

So that's what we do. We go into court. In the court are attorneys and social workers. The caseloads of both the attorneys and the social workers are so immense that they really don't have the time to spend with the child or know too much about the children's lives because of the time restraints. But a CASA volunteer knows more about these children than anyone in the courtroom. And since we provide that information to the court, the court listens to us. The court knows that when a CASA volunteer speaks, he or she is speaking from fact and knows everything about the child. The information we provide weighs heavily in the judge's decision because he or she knows we have done our homework. I think the judges also understand that when a CASA volunteer reports information to the court, it's firsthand information. The CASA volunteer has usually checked and verified or spoken to the people direct-

ly, and it's not from someone else's written report—it's something that they have checked on themselves. The information that a CASA volunteer gives is factual and unbiased since the only responsibility that a CASA volunteer has is to the child. The judges appreciate this, and when they get information from a CASA volunteer, they know it is information they can rely on.

Of all the things we offer, however, the most important thing we give to our CASA kids is consistency. If we promise to show up at 3:00 p.m. on a Wednesday afternoon, we keep that appointment so the child is not disappointed. When we say we're going to be someplace, we are there.

These children that we deal with have been dumped. They've been dumped by parents. They've been dumped by relatives. They've been abused. They've been abandoned. It gets to a point where they don't trust anyone. A CASA volunteer tries to renew that trust, and we succeed in many cases. When a CASA volunteer makes a promise, a CASA volunteer keeps a promise. And this is something these kids are not used to. Knowing that it is us who keep that promise, well, let me tell you, it's a hell of a good feeling. We give children, no matter how small, something that they've never had before— reliability and consistency. One case at a time, very slowly, we do make a difference.

Linda Murphy, Houston, Texas

Do you want to know why I get involved? Think about a two-and-a-half-month-old being raped by her own father. It's shocking, I know—outrageous, sickening, every word you can think of, but it happened. And somebody has to do something about it, be a voice for that child in court, find a way to help that infant survive, find her a home where people can love her and help the scars heal. That's why I work at CASA.

I think about the children all the time. The cases that I've had, I know that the children are in a much better place than they were before, because they are protected now. I protect them. Every night before I go to sleep, I can't help thinking about how the children are now, growing up in entirely different sets of circumstances than they were originally. Through no fault of their own, these children were brutalized, sometimes very early on in their lives. For example, I think not only of the infant who was raped, but her half-sister Brandy, a slender, bright-eyed 5-year-old with a ponytail and a beautiful complexion, who was molested by her stepfather on Mother's Day. I was

I am the voice of a child in court.
I protect her, because through no
fault of her own, children like her
were often brutalized, sometimes
very early on in their lives.
At night before I go to sleep,
I think about how that child
is growing up in an entirely
different set of circumstances
than what she knew—
happier circumstances,
healthier circumstances—
and I find peace knowing I
made a difference.

brought in on the case in July, about a month after the incident occurred. By then, she had been moved to foster care for her safety. I went out to visit the foster family and to meet Brandy so she would grow used to seeing me around. I wanted her to realize I was there to help and gather all the information needed. And even on that first day, even at that first meeting, she felt safe enough to disclose to me that she did not want to go back to her mother, that she wanted to stay with her foster family.

On the surface, you would think Brandy was like any other 5-year-old. She would take me to her bedroom and show me her dolls, her coloring books, and the things she had just brought home from Sunday School. She'd tell me stories about the things in her room and where they came from and which ones she liked the best. And she liked me to read books to her. There was a puppy book that she particularly liked—you know, the picture books that have fuzzy covers you can stroke like real pet fur? So we would read the puppy book. But at the end of the visit, I told her we were going to go into court to talk about what was happening in her life and whether her mother should be allowed to continue seeing her during supervised visits. I asked her, "Is there anything you want me to tell the judge? Anything you want me to tell him, I'll be glad to."

And Brandy looked at me with those bright brown eyes and said, "Tell him I have been good."

Her response took me back a bit, shook me up, because here I had thought she was going to say something about her mother or about living in her new foster home. It just never occurred to me that she already understood what responsibility the judge had in her case. That she understood she was going to be discussed by a judge and that he was going to decide things about her future. Because she had been abused, she had learned that if you talk back to somebody, if you are "bad," it will have some pretty negative repercussions.

"Just tell him that I have been good."

It gets to you, you know. And the case didn't go so well at first. The mother did regain temporary custody of Brandy as well as the baby sister, and sure enough, who comes wandering back but the abusive stepfather. He showed up on a visitation, which of course was totally unauthorized. He shouldn't have been there. Fortunately, during one of the family group therapy sessions, Brandy took her therapist aside and whispered to her that she had seen her perpetrator. After that, things happened fast.

Children's Protective Services (CPS) went out and picked up the children and put them back into foster care. It was a good thing, too, because when CPS picked the kids up, both were covered with mosquito bites. The baby had a urinary tract infection that

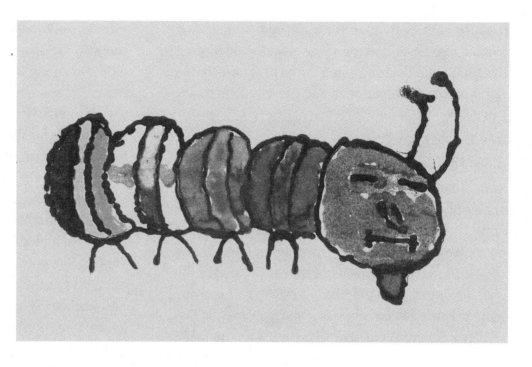

was so severe she would be on antibiotics for a year, and she also needed surgery to restore damage from sexual assault. CPS immediately recommended termination of parental rights.

We had a trial in October that lasted eight working days. First, we had a mistrial because one of the lawyers for the mother said something that was prejudicial. Then we had to go through the whole

sexual abuse scenario. The stepfather claimed innocence throughout his entire testimony, even though the very next day I got a phone call from a former friend of the mother's, telling me that just three months earlier the stepfather had confessed to her husband that he had molested Brandy. Even so, it took a day and a half to get the verdict back, which probably was the most harrowing period of my life, because I felt every minute that went by meant that it wasn't going to come out the way I wanted it to. But finally the decision came down to terminate the rights, both the stepfather's and the mother's rights, just as we had asked.

The relief—I mean, I have never felt so ecstatic. I wanted to shout for joy and burst into tears at the same time. I mean, this woman had the three photographs of her children in front of her on the table the entire time. The stepfather was studiously writing notes. We knew he was low functioning. God knows what he was writing down, but they really played the good parent roles to the hilt. I did feel badly for the mom because I knew she was going to grieve the loss of these children, but there was no way she could bring them up. I personally witnessed her verbally abusing them. We had documented evidence that they had been physically neglected, not to mention the sexual abuse. Still, you feel sad when a family splits up, even though you know it is for the best.

And it has worked out for the best. Both girls now live with the foster parents they started out with and will soon be adopted by them. The couple was childless until the foster mom turned 37 and decided she wanted children. So eventually they received CPS training for foster care and took in these two little girls. Now they have taken in two boys as well. The mom stays home with the kids, and they have a wonderful daddy. I mean, it's just the best of all possible worlds for these children. My goodness, they're taking gymnastics—they're doing beautifully. The little baby is just a sassy little two-and-a-half-year-old. And the four little siblings—of course they are rough and tumble and behave like little puppies and fuss at each other every now and then, but isn't that what happy families do? We were out in the sandbox once, and one of the little boys threw sand at me. He had just newly come into the family and still was learning to cope. But anyway, he was certainly doing something he wasn't supposed to do, and Brandy jumped to my defense.

"This is my advocate," she said to her new brother. "You can't throw sand at her. If you do, I will have my little dog Bugsy throw sand back."

Bugsy is a stuffed dog, but I found the whole thing terribly touching—the way she stood up for me, for herself, and yet also was showing him the rules, the right way to behave.

For me, there is a spiritual joy that comes from knowing that things are going to be better for these children. And it's a great gift to me, but it's amazing to be in a position where I can do that for somebody else. It's typical, maybe, to do unto others or whatever. I never thought about it in terms of my children. I'd really want my children to be rescued by somebody competent if they were in any kind of danger. And in a way, these children are my own children. I mean, isn't that what we are supposed to do, take care of one another? Take care of those people who need help?

Premelia Lindor, Manchester, New Hampshire

I have worked all my adult life to help kids, first volunteering in my children's schools and some parent aid work. But when I retired, I wanted to go one step further and do something that was a little more involved, more challenging and more one-on-one with children. And so I found CASA. And yes, it is challenging, especially since you have to make your way through the labyrinth of the court system. But it also makes you feel very well-educated about our court and justice system, which adds a whole new dimension to my understanding of how government works.

The system does need a lot of work. Not so much the people who work there, the lawyers and family services staff—for the most part, they are very hardworking, dedicated people. Financially, there is just so much need. More money for the kids, more money for the caseworkers, more money to hire more administrators to handle all the paperwork. Oh yeah, and the judges. The judges are great. They hold our CASA reports in their hands, and always refer to them first and foremost and nearly always end up going with our recommendations. They

Until a 7-year-old child says to you, "What would my mommy and me do without you? You're the one who's going to get us back together," you have no idea just how important you are, just how much you serve a purpose in this world.

know we are volunteers, and we make it possible for the system to work, so they really put a lot of stock in what we say and what we know, and show us a lot of appreciation and encouragement.

I remember my first case involved a mother and her 7-year-old daughter, Misty. The mother had been addicted to drugs and alcohol for a number of years, so the state finally made the decision to place her daughter in a foster home where she would be better cared for. But when Misty was finally taken from her, she hit rock bottom.

What is it they say about when you are at your lowest, you have no place to go but up? Well, I think that is what happened here. She realized she had lost her child and she was really discouraged. Intimidated by the system, she was very angry and defensive. She couldn't understand why this had happened to her. I tried to get her to understand that it was happening to her daughter, too—because of her own behavior, her daughter would suffer. So that was when I began to really understand that to serve a child best, you sometimes have to serve as an advocate for the mother as much as for the child.

I must have gotten through to her, because within a year's time, she had turned her life around, moved to a new location, gave up all her old friends and went through some drug and alcohol counseling, and got a new job and a nice new apartment. She worked really, really hard to change, and I could see her struggle. Sometimes she would come up against the system, be talking with the judge and family services, and I could see that she was irritated, angry that they didn't see she had changed, and I would just motion to her to stay calm. And most of the time, she held her tongue, even though she wanted to throw a tantrum.

The sad part was that while the mother was getting her life together, Misty had already been in and out of four foster homes. She missed her mother and became so depressed nobody seemed to be able to handle it. At first, the doctors were overmedicating her with things that weren't necessary, so I stepped in and took her on the doctor's visits myself. It's not that I didn't trust the foster parents; they gave her a beautiful room and lots of attention. But I wanted to get all the information for myself, so I talked to the doctor, and the foster parents, and her teachers, and

got a lot more details about how she was responding or not responding, and finally got her on the right antidepressant. That made a big difference. And just about that time, her mother began visiting her consistently. So, she was beginning to see some hope. But those first seven or eight months or so were difficult—she was just broken. And I was real worried that we were going to lose her before the reunification. In fact, I was so worried about her initially, that even though we are not encouraged to do so, I gave her my home phone number.

And because of her many different placements, I became the one stable element in Misty's life. There were times when she called me just because she needed to talk to someone and she couldn't contact her mother. I could see it made a big difference in her life. And when I would come to visit her, she would grin from ear-to-ear and give me a big hug.

She once said to me, "What would my mommy and me do without you? You're the only one we like. You know, you're the one who's going to get us back together."

I think that too often on cases everybody else has to act so professional that the families feel intimidated. I think that a CASA volunteer serves more as a personal contact, somebody who children can feel safe with, who they can feel comfortable with, who they can swear with if they have to, or let their guard down with if they have to.

And it's not so much that I think I offered the mother anything extraordinary. I just listened, and I tried to arrange visits with doctors or therapists and made sure that the social worker visited regularly. And of course I spoke up for both the mother and the child in court. The mother already had a lot going for her, but nobody had ever bothered to tell her that, so she didn't believe it. She was bright, she was pretty, she was scared to death, and I think she just needed someone to tell her you can do it. You are the one who's going to have to do it.

She told me herself a number of times that she just didn't know how to do it. She didn't know she could really make different choices. She just never had that kind of role model in her life. But she turned it around anyway, and now she and Misty are back together.

Misty has grown so much since then. She is involved in school, takes all these extracurriculars, plays the violin, participates in 4H. They have a meticulous little apartment and they are best friends—they are just so there for each other. And every few months or so, they send a card or invite me to a birthday party, so I know they are doing well. To this day, I don't think her mom's got a man in her life. I don't think that's important to her. I think Misty is her number one priority.

Oh, it's a wonderful thing to see, knowing that you really made such a difference. To know you have a purpose in this world. And for me personally, this case and working with CASA was a lifesaver because I had just lost my own daughter in a car accident, and you go through a couple of months when you really don't know if you're going to survive. You really don't know if you want to survive. And then you have these little voices calling you, these children calling you on the phone, needing your help.

You go to visit them and you see it in their eyes. You know how much they need you and how much they depend on you, and you think to yourself, these kids need me right now. And more than anything, you need to feel you have a purpose. People don't always realize what having a purpose gives you. CASA gives me back a lot more than I could ever hand out.

Beverly Tuttle, Porcupine, South Dakota

I was a social worker for the office of the Indian Child Welfare Act when I first became involved with CASA. As a social worker, I certainly felt that I was making a difference, but I remember the first time I sat in a courtroom and watched them give a child from our reservation to a non-Indian family. Clearly the child needed a safe place to go, and I'm sure the family who took him planned to care for him, but I kept thinking how I would feel if I was the child—that a bunch of people I've met only once or twice, who were from a different background and a different culture, were making decisions about my future. And I became really emotional and started crying, because I felt like there were some real racial issues to deal with, and that was when I realized how our children needed somebody to speak for them. That was back in 1992, and I've been a CASA volunteer ever since.

Certainly my social work experience helps, but the training you receive from CASA is really important, because it helps you know what you really need to pinpoint or focus on. That means focusing on the

Being a CASA is like opening my heart to allow those who are hurt to heal.

total child's welfare, on what the child needs at the time, and what she will need long-term. It means reviewing and carefully investigating the child's file, gleaning as much information about the family as possible, in the hopes that maybe you can bring the family back together. After all, that's what our reservation is, not so much a village but a family, an extended family, where we share the same land base and in some cases blood relations. So the way I view it, being a CASA is like opening my heart to allow those who are hurt to heal.

Here at the Pine Ridge Reservation, those are the main things we focus on—helping the children relate back to who they are, their identity, using all of our natural resources to help children back into a sense of belonging. Even if it is not with their birthparents, we need to connect them with somebody who can give them that feeling, that compassion, that belonging. That they are Native American. That they are Lakota. They matter to us. They belong with us and their community.

Back in 1999, I got a call from the CASA coordinator, who told me of a case at the Juvenile Detention Center in Kiowa that concerned two ado-

lescent sisters from the reservation, Marie and Angela. They had been incarcerated for reasons unknown and needed someone to see what was what. So I drove down there. The most disheartening thing for me at the time was that when we interviewed those two little girls for the first time, they had no idea why they were even there, no understanding of what had happened to them. They were withdrawn, and it was very hard to get them to express their feelings. Finally, I asked them, "What would you like to have happen for you?" They said that all they wanted was to go back to their mother, who was a quadriplegic.

Turns out that the girls had been staying home from school to care for their sick mother. The landlord saw the kids home from school and called the truancy officer, and they came and put them in JD. Right off the bat, they were labeled as trouble. And when you're labeled like that, you've got a reputation, and it becomes very hard for you to fight what it says about you on a piece of paper. In this case, the children just wanted to care for their ailing mother. So by the time I met Marie and Angela, they had sort of shut down those instinctual survival emotions you need to cope. They were just so overwhelmed by what was happening to them that they lost interest in the time of day. They lost interest in who was looking out for them. They just sat there in the juvenile facility, waiting. I think they had given up hope. And so we, as CASA volunteers, went in there, and we tried to revive them. And we did. We arranged for them to come back to the Pine Ridge Reservation and to have someone care for them until their mother was released from the hospital.

And then, almost by accident, I made an important discovery. I was working on one of my cases for the district in Porcupine and ran into another volunteer. We would sometimes swap stories and share experiences. So I told him about these two Lakota girls who were from Colorado. I told him that their mother was sick and we were trying to track down other members of the family, the father or a grandmother. He got really quiet all of a sudden, and said that he had a little girl who was living in Colorado. So we connected the stories, and it turns out that he was the father of one of the little girls—they had the same mom, but different dads. So he was one of the girl's fathers, and we arranged to have them all meet.

Eventually, their mother came out of the hospital and they went back to live with her, but I understand that the father is still very much involved in that little girl's life. Marie told me later that she is really proud to have a father who cares for her. But it just shows you how cut off many of our people are from one another. After they leave the reservation, they get into trouble, don't know who to turn to for help, can't always afford to stay in touch with other relatives. They get lost, and for a people who, between brothers and sisters and aunts and uncles and great-aunts and great-uncles, may be related to a hundred people, it is a tragedy to see them cut off.

There are too many negative labels placed on Indian people. We know that some of our people suffer from alcoholism. We know that there's a lot of sexual abuse, that there's a lot of violence. But not everyone is like that—it's sort of like saying that all white people are blonde or only care about money.

Those stereotypes live on in the courts, so without advocacy from Indian people in that courtroom, the tendency in the past has been to place the children in non-Indian homes. But CASA is working to change that. We are bringing our Indian children back into our Indian families. Because that's where they belong. I don't mean to say that placing children in non-Indian homes is a bad thing. Clearly these are caring, loving people, but I think it should be the second choice—only if we can't find relatives who are willing and capable of caring for them. These children are our future. Without them, our people, the Lakota, will disappear.

Mary Kilgour, Gainesville, Florida

Let me get this out of the way first, because I want to talk about the kids more than about myself. I was one of those kids who could have benefited from a CASA volunteer when I was young. I lived in an orphanage as a teenager, but they didn't have CASA volunteers back then. Of course, there were some adults who took an interest in me before my parents died, such as a couple of teachers, a librarian, even a neighbor. But when I finally ended up in a home for girls run by nuns, the head nun had a very positive influence on me and got me on the right path.

CASA volunteers don't simply serve as role models. As a court appointed child advocate, I represent a child in court to make sure all decisions are made in the best interests of that child and that child's future. We do this not just by filling in the blanks in standard forms the way bureaucrats tend to do, but by getting to know the child on a personal level. That means getting to know his or her family, maybe teachers, doctors, anyone who can help provide a complete picture of what the child is about and what he or she is up against.

A kid coming from a troubled home doesn't necessarily learn things automatically. I remember how when I was a teenager, after my parents died, I would sit on a bus and observe how normal adults interacted and behaved, so that I could copy what they did.

Things have definitely changed since I was in the juvenile justice system back in the 1950s. In some ways, they've gotten more protective of the child—the abuse laws, for instance—but at the same time the whole Miranda rights issue has made it more of an adversarial relationship. The court may be looking out for the child, but it also seems to treat the child more like a criminal. With my first CASA case, they brought the child into juvenile court in chains from the detention center, and it tore at my heart. And while I don't claim to be an expert and don't understand all the reasons why the courts have become this way, treating a 12-year-old child—who may have gotten himself into trouble in a foster home—as a dangerous criminal, dragging him into court in handcuffs and leg chains, was an absolute shock. On the other hand, the people in the state attorney's office, the ones I've dealt with, are all competent. They're compassionate and overworked, but they seem to know what they're doing. And by and large, the Children and Family Services people are competent, but they're so overwhelmed and have such small budgets that they shortchange these children in many cases. It's not their fault, though,

because the state legislature doesn't equip them with adequate funds.

That's where we as CASA volunteers come in. We don't have to worry about politics much; we're pretty free to do what we think is sensible. I think maybe we just have more freedom and certainly more time than a government worker to interact with a child as a human being. I can speak on that since I spent 29 years working in a bureaucracy as a Foreign Service officer. So it's ironic I guess, me finding the value of working without a lot of rules.

So about this child, Jimmy, the one in chains. He's a handsome young boy. He has one dimple, which he likes to flash. He's got pretty blue eyes and rosy cheeks. Give him a couple more years, and he'll be a real charmer. He's husky, would make a great football player, though baseball is his favorite sport. From the physical abuse he received when he was young, he developed posttraumatic stress disorder; the same condition that some of the Vietnam vets suffered from being around so much death and violence. But this was a young boy, only 12 when I first got his case, and he had already been away from his natural home for several years. So Jimmy was angry, acting out, behaving self-destructively, doing things to get kicked out of foster homes, misbehaving to the point of having to be hospitalized in a crisis stabilization unit. Even though he's bright and could handle the schoolwork, he would act up in class—doing anything to get attention in a negative way. So he has been in a variety of different foster homes over the years, and his last one would have been a great placement for him, but he had a physical confrontation with his foster father, and that was the end of that. I asked Jimmy later if he was sorry since he genuinely seemed to like and relate well to that foster father, and he said he was. He just doesn't seem able to control his emotions. But he is definitely improving with lots of therapy. I'll get to that in a moment.

So here was this disruptive boy in the middle of puberty, who had been in and out of crisis stabilization centers, in and out of foster care, even spent time in a home for runaways. My top priority was finding him the right kind of environment in which to live.

It wasn't an easy task. I felt my biggest role as a child advocate in this particular case was to complain, be a thorn in the side of Children's Protective Services and the court system, to make sure he wouldn't fall through the cracks. When the children are older, have more of a history of violence, of being disruptive, I don't think the system is very sympathetic. So back into a foster home he would go, and then he would have to leave because his behavior had deteriorated, and there were just too many kids in a single home for his behavior to be tolerated. And I would screech. In my reports to the court, I would just say over and over again, "The adults in this child's life must do something!" And I mean I was really screeching at CPS; I sort of caught hold of the boy's anger. Fortunately, the judge saw the need, too. She had compassion and was willing to crack some heads. She got Jimmy assigned to a group home with an excellent therapy program, even though the state said there was no more money. They appealed her opinion, or judgment I guess it's called. But I liked this judge; she was smart and more than that, she cared what happened to this kid even more than she cared about her career. She knew it would take many months before the appeal would be heard, and in the meantime the boy would be getting the care and help he needed. I guess the reason CPS appealed her ruling was that residential treatment centers cost a lot more money than the typical foster home, so they had to take money away from some other child who wasn't under the eye of this particular judge. And that's where we get back to budget issues again and the legislature not providing enough funding for this problem in our society.

Hopefully, we've gotten to Jimmy in time, put him on the right path, so he can have a chance at a good life. Already I can see of a lot of positive changes in him. When I first met him, if I touched him, just lightly put my hand on his arm, he would pull away snarling, "Don't touch me!" He did this with every adult he encountered. He just didn't want human contact. Well, I went to see him last night at the group home, brought him some candy, and all on his own, he hugged me. He said, "This is just a hug," and he hugged me. For him to initiate contact like that is a major accomplishment. Another major accomplishment is that at 14, he is finally starting to read. Of course, he knew how to read—he just never did. Maybe a lot of teenage boys are like that, but it is unfortunate. Reading can open so many doors. So I gave him the first two volumes of *Harry Potter* and

he started reading them. He told me last night that he had lost the second volume before finishing it. He was upset because he knew he was going to get the third volume for his birthday, and he didn't want to start the third book until he had found out what happened at the end of *Harry Potter and the Chamber of Secrets*. I was pleased to see how much the books had come to matter to him. So even though he will always have his ups and downs, to me his reading is a wonderful step. Thanks to regular therapy and the stability and the continuity he's getting from the group home, he is slowly overcoming some of his issues.

He's just generally gotten better at learning social skills. He had to learn those. A kid coming from a troubled home doesn't necessarily learn those things automatically. I remember when I was a teenager, after my parents died, I would sit on a bus and observe how normal adults interacted and behaved so that I could copy what they did. That is how this kid has to learn what is appropriate behavior—step-by-step.

Even though I didn't want to talk about my life, the truth is that serving as a CASA advocate has encouraged me to examine my own childhood in much more detail than I ever really had in the past. In fact, I've started writing about it. I've written an autobiographical novel aimed at young adults and am now looking to have it published. Working with CASA has made me look back at how I got on the right path, what helped me, and what I might do to help these kids get on their own right paths. And though society has changed from when I was a kid, I think that essentially kids still need the same things they needed back then, such as love, connection with others, and stability. The whole process has not only made me a more sensitive CASA volunteer, but it's made me a more sensitive person in general. It's made me hopeful for these kids because I looked back at my own life, at how and where I started out, and realized that I have a Horatio Alger story of my own. I try to encourage these kids that if I could do it, they can too.

Dago Benavidez, Salem, Oregon

I have a real connection with neglected or forgotten children. I come from a Latino family of migrant farmers, and we used to travel from state to state, following the harvests. When I was a little boy, I remember children who, having been abused at home, would look forward to school because it served as a kind of safe haven from their parents. The teachers didn't know about this because the kids didn't really have anyone looking out for them who would share that type of thing with the school. But I knew it because they were friends of mine, and I was aware of the hardships they were going through at home. It's these personal experiences and the fact that some of these Latino children are falling by the wayside that got me involved in CASA.

It is very important that I get involved because I'm bilingual, and these kids or their caregivers often don't understand or speak English. Not only are the children scared about what's happening to them or where they are going to end up as they make their way through the family court system, but also there's no one there to explain to them

The judges respect our recommendations because we're speaking for the child... They know we aren't there out of self-interest, or to fight for our own agenda. We're just doing what's good for the child. As a Latino, I think it's encouraging the way things are going with the judicial system— Latinos getting involved with helping Latino children.

what's going on. And with the Latino population growing by leaps and bounds, it stands to reason that more Latino children are going to be in the system, needing help and guidance from someone who can speak Spanish.

One such case that I've been working on is coming to a positive and happy conclusion. When I first met Rosie, she was very much an introvert. Because her mother was moderately mentally retarded and also suffered from epilepsy, she took heavy medications when she was pregnant. As a result, Rosie was born with fingernails that weren't fully formed. Nobody was aware of this situation until the grandmother shared that information with me in Spanish. I asked the Services to Children and Families (SCF) worker if they had done a psychological evaluation on the child, and he said no. So I requested that they do one. The psychologist had Rosie play games until she felt comfortable and started to open up. It turns out Rosie had always been introverted because she was embarrassed about not having fingernails like everyone else. She talked about how she would hide her hands and fingers whenever she was in public because she didn't want anyone to see them.

The psychologist said the best thing for me to do would be to get Rosie into Head Start to help her socialize with other children her own age. It took a lot of work to get her enrolled because of the amount of paperwork and the fact that her grandmother could not speak or read English. So I helped her grandmother with the paperwork, and after a couple of months, we were able to get her enrolled.

Now Rosie is thriving. She's living with her grandmother, and every time I go over to their home, her face lights up with a smile when she sees me. It's just such a great reward to see this big, beautiful smile.

I also help the grandmother whenever I can because helping the family helps the child. For instance, the grandmother called me once, upset because SCF informed her that her apartment was not certified, and that she couldn't adopt Rosie until she lived in a certified residence. I contacted the grandmother's landlord and learned that he was remodeling a rental house that he owned. I explained the situation to him—that I was a CASA volunteer and that I was trying to get this child adopted by her grandmother, but the adoption couldn't go through until the family lived in a certified residence. As a result, he agreed to rent the house to Rosie's grandmother and SCF helped pay the deposit on the house. So now Rosie and her grandmother live in a beautiful home, and we're moving forward with the adoption process.

A year into Rosie's case, her mother had another child, a little boy. Because of the mother's mental condition, which made it impossible for her to care properly for the baby, he was immediately placed with a paternal uncle. As a CASA volunteer, I made sure that the judge saw and approved my recommendations that the two children had visitation rights. Because of that, I don't feel bad about the children being in two separate homes because they are with relatives, and the relatives make sure that the children see each other on a regular basis.

Through this whole process, I find the court system really supportive of the work CASA volunteers do—they believe in the CASA program. It's really gratifying that they view CASA volunteers as professionals looking out for the best interests of the children. The judges always make a point of asking the CASA volunteers if they have anything further they

would like to add at the end of the proceedings. Judges also ask us questions about the children and their families before they make decisions. I truly feel we are making a big difference when we deal with the judicial system because people have a sincere interest in what we have to say.

The judges respect our recommendations because we're speaking for the child, and because they are the ones who assigned us to that particular child in the first place. They know we aren't there out of self-interest, nor do we have our own agenda. We're just doing what's good for the child. And as a Latino, I think it's encouraging the way things are going with the judicial system. The courts have become aware of the need for Latinos to get involved with Latino children.

As Latinos, it's our responsibility to advocate for these children. It's also important that Latino men take a role because children in the Latino community and culture look up to us—a respect we have to live up to. If we show them a positive direction when they're young, those children can go on to be productive members of their communities.

When I first started as a CASA volunteer, I knew I wanted to advocate for children. But it becomes more real and tangible the more you do it. It—the work, the kids—just grows on you. The rewards aren't monetary, but more spiritual. The more you see the need for CASA, the more you want to do.

Linda Warfield, Phoenix, Arizona

I am not sure why I became a CASA volunteer, or what motivated me to seek a volunteer position to advocate for children. My husband and I already had our hands full raising three daughters, and on top of that, I was working toward a degree I had put on hold to start a family. Whatever the reason, I remember walking into the training and feeling like I was in way over my head. As I listened to the trainers speak, I wondered why so many children were removed from their families and what I could do to change this scenario.

After my initial training, I was asked to review some cases to see if any interested me. As I sat alone in a small room, I stared at the pile of folders in front of me. As each folder revealed a story of a child, I thought I was reading fiction. How could this happen to some small and innocent child? I became particularly interested in two children, a brother and sister, who had been removed from their home on Christmas night. A night when most children, after a day of family, toys, and a turkey dinner are tucked into warm beds, with smiles on their faces,

Being a CASA pulls at your heartstrings and at the same time gives you strength to fight for even the smallest thing.

and memories of all the festivities that peacefully carry them into dreamland.

Unfortunately the real world of domestic violence, spurred by drug abuse, sent the mother and her two children running down a busy street late into the night. For these children, Christmas memories included a homeless shelter and tears of fear.

As I continued reading, I realized this incident happened two years prior and the original CASA volunteer had removed herself due to personal reasons. These two children, now living in foster care, had lost their parents, their home, their CASA volunteer, and all they knew in their world, in a short period of time. As I closed the file, I decided I would do whatever I could to change their lives for the better. Aspirations filled my head as I announced to my coordinator that I wanted this case. She completed the paperwork and asked if I had any questions. Questions? My mind went in 50 directions, but the only words that came out my mouth were, "Where do I begin?"

After calling all parties involved, I made an appointment to meet the children. Jena and Joe were full of questions like who I was, did I know their parents, and when would they go home. My big plans for these children started that day with small steps and short answers.

Drugs and domestic violence are intertwined in the lives of so many children. Childhood concepts become adolescent beliefs if not explained. These parents wanted Jena and Joe back, but would continue to use drugs. Court orders to take parenting skills classes were initially obeyed, but attendance dwindled quickly. Drug testing was easily forgotten, and the domestic violence continued according to police records, although denied by all parties. The parents were so caught up in their lifestyle that even the desire to be reunited with their children became second to their needs.

I remember driving Jena and Joe to the park one day. We were passed by a police car with its lights and sirens blaring. When I looked in my rearview mirror, both children were crouched down in their seats, with their eyes closed. I pulled over quickly and asked what was wrong. Sheepishly Jena replied, "They are the ones that take you away from your parents and put you in baby jail." This was reality for these children.

Being a CASA volunteer stirs you up emotionally, and at the same time gives you strength to fight for even the smallest thing. As I started to understand just what it was to advocate for these children, I began to look at the real world and myself more clearly. I was very happy as I watched Jena be successfully adopted, but it was a bittersweet moment, as Joe had been placed in a new long-term foster care, and they would no longer live together.

When I visited him after his return from the family that he thought he had become a member of, I saw firsthand how a spirit can be broken. Here he was again in a child shelter, while his sister got adopted. He could not understand why. He asked me to tell his family that he would not get mad again and hit anyone. He said he promised to do what he was told and listen to his new mom and dad. Then he asked me to call his real parents and see if they would pick him up and take him home, but they had left the state and were nowhere to be found. Abandoned, alone, and with a broken heart, we sat together on a pair of swings at the playground near the crisis shelter.

I advocated hard from that point forward to get changes made in his life. Resolving his mental health issues, medical issues, evaluations, anger management issues, and finding him a careful placement became my goals. I had the opportunity to stand in front of the juvenile judge and ask for what I believed the child needed. I made phone calls and did legwork to help the case managers. Most of all, I served as a constant figure to Joe, so he had someone he trusted to call when he was upset or just to tell me about a book he read. I became not a new face in his ever-changing world, but someone who always showed up when I said I would. I was the person who sent a card on his birthday and listened to whatever he had to say.

There have been other CASA children that I have been involved with, who have been provided with a future and are doing well. Unfortunately, not all foster children are adopted.

But with my help, Joe is now with a loving foster family where he can stay as long as he wants. He is learning to control his temper when things do not go his way. He is learning to attach to members of his family, something he never learned as a child. He is

a gifted student and a kind spirit. Luckily, he has a wonderful family now that helps him over these hurdles and wants to give him a wonderful future.

As for me, I realized that making a difference can happen in small ways. Each little step helped put two children on the road of life where they had been left by the wayside. With Jena and Joe as my teachers, I no longer try to tackle giant situations all at once. I take time to sit in the park and enjoy what is around me, seek simple solutions, and accept that even happy endings can be bittersweet.

As I mentor new CASA volunteers now, I often remember what it was like for me. When I listen to questions they ask like "Where do I begin?" I smile to myself. Being a CASA volunteer means reaching out to a small hand that needs holding. It means giving hope. It means working toward the future of a child who has no future unless someone says, "I will make a difference."

Donna Ratcliffe, Seminole County, Florida

I now take pride and am fulfilled by the smaller things in life, because what seems small to you might actually be a great accomplishment for an abused or neglected child.

There is one particular child I remember. It was sort of an atypical case for me because generally I work on criminal cases in which a parent or caregiver has caused a child severe injury. But this case was more about neglect and abandonment. When I met Sean, he was with his kid sister at a shelter. He was 8 years old, very quiet, and I had to pause to collect myself when I first saw him because he had severe burns all over his lower face, neck, arms, and chest. I learned that prior to being abandoned at the age of 5, he felt such great despair, that he set himself on fire with a match. Shortly thereafter, his parents abandoned him and his sister, and the children came into the system. While his sister was adopted rather quickly, Sean had many psychological issues—as well as his burn marks, which could be very off-putting—indicating that he was not a strong candidate for adoption. No one was willing to adopt a "problem"

I now take pride and am fulfilled by the smaller things in life, because what may seem small to you can actually be a great accomplishment for an abused or neglected child.

child, which just made matters worse since he wondered why people wanted his sister but not him. So he went through several foster homes, including therapeutic foster care.

At the same time, he probably had seven or eight different caseworkers during a 10-year period, so I was the only constant in his life. I made sure that no matter who his caseworker was, he stayed in long-term counseling. You have to argue for this, of course, since counseling costs money, which is why each time his case came up, I went into court and made sure he got what he needed, at least as much as we could give a burned kid with no stability who was labeled a problem child.

But then the unexpected happened. I think that is what I have learned most about being a CASA volunteer—to expect the unexpected. We arranged for Sean to be profiled on Wednesday's Child, a television news show that runs once a week in Orlando to introduce a child and let people know he or she is available for adoption. A woman who saw the program had also been a burn victim, and I guess her heart went out to him. So she contacted the state's Department of Children and Family Services to see

if she could meet him. Sea World was sponsoring a special one-day foster child/adoptive child program to bring all the potential parents and children together. I took Sean to meet her, and it was really great. She decided that she wanted to adopt him. It seemed ideal, especially when we learned that she was a family therapist.

So Sean went into her home for an adjustment period prior to adoption. As I said, you need to expect the unexpected because even though she really wanted him and loved him, things quickly deteriorated. You have to realize that this was the first situation where someone really showed Sean that he was wanted. And he ran from that. It frightened him, so he started doing a lot of really bizarre things, playing with fire again and destructive things. So back he went into a residential treatment center home, where he stayed for a year and a half before he stabilized. But when he came out, he learned that she had stuck by him—she still wanted him after all that time and trouble. She stuck by him and I stuck by him—I mean this had been like eight years at this point, seven to eight years. And in the end, we all went down to the courthouse, and she finally adopted him. It was a big deal; even Governor Chiles was there. So never let anyone tell you there are no happy endings.

Sean's nearly 18 now and in the wrestling pro-gram at high school and he plays football. He's got excellent grades. I stay in contact with him on a semi-regular basis to make sure things are okay. He called me a couple of months ago to ask me if I would be his mentor for a special project that he was doing in school. It was his senior class project, and he decided to do it on adoption. And he called me to be his men-tor. The way his call made me feel was beyond words, because even though I've dealt with cases worse than his, even more severe cases of abuse, this child had struggled for so long, had setback after set-back. This poor brave kid had to go to Cincinnati every year to have his skin graft stretched because as a child grows, the scar tissue doesn't expand. Yet he still believed and knew I wanted to help. I felt privi-leged to be one of the few people in his life who did not give up on him, and he knew it. I fully anticipate being invited to his wedding someday. I see myself buying baby gifts when he gets married and has a child of his own. I mean, I will be in this child's life

forever, and that's the biggest reward that I think I've ever had, earning and keeping his trust, that he relied on me all those years and remembered how I helped.

And he is unusual, too, because you don't always get verbal accolades from the children you help, especially the younger ones who don't completely understand what is going on. Either that, or they just want to move forward with their new lives and their new families, and that's okay with me, because being told thank you is not why I do it.

I do it because when I was a children's Sunday School director at my church I saw many very privi-leged children who had everything, all their needs met, positive nurturing, and it tugged at my heart that, at the same time, there was a whole facet of our county's population, especially in my own area, who were just falling through the cracks. I would read in the paper about cases that had gone bad, children who were hurt, had even in some cases lost their lives, and I knew I had to give back.

I've had many children adopted into fine, fine homes. I've had extremely abusive situations, where children were seriously injured and the perpetrator has gone away and will never be a part of the child's life again or is doing prison time. I think how CASA has changed me is that I've learned that you can't handle cases in a cookie cutter fashion, can't control all outcomes. Maybe in business you can, but like I said earlier, when you work with children, the unexpected is usually the thing that happens.

Like the children, I have to learn what is appropriate for a CASA volunteer to do. Although I am relentless in court and I don't make any bones about speaking up and I don't care who likes me and who doesn't, I do want the child to like me. And I want to be a soft pillow, provide a cushy feeling for that child. I want to come off like the sweetest, nicest, most fun-loving, let's-sing-songs-and-go-have-ice-cream kind of person. That's what I want to be to the child. So to the childen, I want to be a friend, someone who they know they can come to if they need something. But I am also in an authoritative position because my other job is to fight for those kids, even if what I am fighting for is something they themselves don't think they want, but I know they need. I mean, I'll fight anybody I have to and speak my mind and do a thor-

ough investigation and write a 10-page report if necessary. I interview anyone and everyone I can possibly think of who is involved with the child's well-being. Maybe I use my interview information or maybe not, but at least it gives me the total picture. So it's a multiple-task job. Most importantly, I am the voice for that child in court, and I need to give accurate information to the court because as much of a great pal as I might be to that child, if I don't do my job concisely and persistently in court, with accurate information, a ruling could come down that could affect that child for the rest of his or her life. What good is my being a buddy to that kid if I don't help him or her in court? So that is my utmost goal—to bring about the ruling that is going to be most beneficial to that child. And it may not just be my opinion. I try to get a consensus of what the authorities think, of what the mental health professionals feel, and take that information and be unbiased. That's why judges trust us—they know we speak for the child.

So now I take pride and am fulfilled by much smaller things. Because even if something seems like a small accomplishment to you, like learning to tie your shoes for the first time, even learning how to hug, it could be a huge accomplishment for them. I'm in my 40s, and I have a list of things at which I've succeeded. But my happiness stems from theirs, because the small things that the children have done and accomplished have now become big accomplishments for me, too.

Stephanie O'Shieles, Houston, Texas

I've always wanted to help others—felt the need to serve. I had a great childhood. I was lucky. Even though I came from divorced parents, a lot of kids in my age group did, so it didn't seem like a big deal. I remember as a teenager in high school, looking at some of the other students around me who came from bad homes or who struggled in school, and I wished there was something I could do that would make their lives better. But when you're 12, you don't really know what to do, so you decide that when you get old enough, then you can help. And I guess I followed through because when I graduated from college I wanted to be a social worker. But then I heard about CASA from my aunt, who had been a child advocate volunteer for three or four years. So after working at a variety of nonprofit agencies, trying to find my niche, I came to work for CASA. Staff members aren't required to take on cases, but every day I heard about kids in need and every day I saw volunteers giving their time to help, and I wanted to do it, too. And even though I'm no longer employed by CASA, I'm still a volunteer.

I feel like a private investigator.
I feel like Santa Claus.
I'm a mediator.
Sometimes I am simply a friend, a playmate.
You play so many roles as a CASA volunteer.

Here's the reason why I do it. It's because of cases like Gabrielle's. Can you imagine that on the day you are born, the state takes you into custody because they already fear for your health and safety? That's what happened to Gabrielle. Thanks to her mom's own addictions, Gabrielle tested positive for both cocaine and HIV at birth. So, even though Children's Protective Services went ahead and let Gabrielle's mother take her home from the hospital—after giving the mother instructions on how to care for an HIV child—CPS checked on her to make sure she was okay. And sure enough, when Gabrielle was just 8 months old, both her mother and father were arrested. Turns out the father ran a robbery ring in Houston and would follow elderly people around, beat them up, and take their money. He didn't drink or smoke or do drugs—he just considered robbing people his job. Meanwhile, Gabby's mother was being investigated for prostitution when she was picked up for her part in the robberies. So with both parents in jail, as an infant, Gabby went into an emergency shelter for children with HIV. The first day she got there, she had a thorough examination. Her white blood cell count was very high, which meant that probably nobody had bothered to give her the medication. It's a tragedy because if she had gotten her medication regularly, if her mom had given it to her, Gabby would only have had a 7% chance of contracting HIV. Now, it was too late.

And she had a horrible case of diaper rash that wouldn't go away. But what bothered me the most was that she didn't really seem to be bonded with anyone. Now this was a gorgeous biracial child, with a light brown complexion and very soft, curly hair, and eyes that lit up a room, and a smile that nobody could resist. She would walk up to any person she saw and say, "How are you? Let's sing this song." She's one of those children who dominates a room. She would have everybody in the room staring at her. But that also scared me a little because she would walk up to anyone, let anyone hug her, but she didn't have a particular affinity for one person. She had never learned to bond.

When I first met her, she had been at the shelter probably a month or so, and one of the volunteers who worked there, a single woman in her late 20s, fell in love with her and wanted to be her foster parent. This woman's life was just a regular life. She went to work, she went home, she hung out with her friends, did her volunteer work, and was in the Junior League. She saw Gabrielle at the shelter and said, "I have to take her home."

While the system was processing the papers so she could take Gabrielle, this woman would go to the shelter every night and tuck in Gabrielle. Night after night she did this because it was taking a while to get the case through the system. The birth mother was released early from jail on good behavior, and she asked the judge to give her more time to try to get her daughter back. She promised she would change, do anything to have her child back. She told him she had found God and that taking care of her family was her top priority. This mother could talk, let me tell you. She could convince you that the sky was orange. And not just any orange, but the most radiant orange it could ever be. She had that effect on people, and that was our biggest obstacle—the court really believed her, wanted to believe her. I wanted to believe her too, but our research showed that, in the past, she would clean up her act, get a job, an apartment, go to counseling and rehab, but would

relapse into her old lifestyle the minute anything became too difficult or too stressful. So we fought in court to terminate parental rights, because we knew that was the only way Gabby would ever have a life. The mother herself had HIV, but that was not the reason we wanted termination—we wanted parental rights terminated because the mother didn't remember to give Gabby her medication, and for an HIV-infected child, that medication is the difference between life and death. Finally, because the judge truly listened to what we had to say, the birthmother and birthfather's rights were terminated when Gabby was 3, and Gabby got to go live with the foster mother.

So it's a happy ending. I mean, it makes me feel fantastic. It makes me feel like there's hope in this world for those you thought were hopeless. That there is a future for this child. I try to imagine her at 18, being able to stand up for herself and how everyone will want to be around such a wonderful, gorgeous creature. But then I get sad, too, and hope that she will live to be 18, that AIDS will not take her away from her new family and home too soon. But I have the satisfaction of knowing that I helped give her a chance, that no matter how long she lives, she will grow up in a safe and loving environment, something all children should have.

That's what being a CASA volunteer means to me. Sometimes when I'm working on cases, some of the lawyers and even the parents, they look at a person my age, still in her 20s, and they seem to question my right to be there. Sort of like saying that because I am so young and don't yet have children of my own, I have no right or reference point for making the recommendations that I do. But in some way, not having children yet may be better because I don't make it a personal issue. I assume all mothers love their own children and would never hurt them. So I feel I can be objective. I feel I can speak for the best interests of the child. And the judges seem to think so, too, because they are always very responsive to what I say, which is very, very empowering. I feel like I'm being heard. That the child is being heard. In court, I'm a mediator, an advocate. Outside court, sometimes I feel like a private investigator. Sometimes I feel like Santa Claus. As a volunteer, I feel like I play so many roles. Sometimes I am there to be the friend, to be the playmate, to be the mentor.

But above all, I am there. I am there in that child's life when other people just come and go.

Afterword

After reading these powerful, personal stories, you may wonder if becoming a CASA volunteer is for you. You may think you need a special background or training to become a volunteer. Just ask Steve and Sue Forstadt, and they will tell you, "It's all just about caring and common sense."

It's also about listening. Our volunteers provide essential information to judges about a child's situation and best interests, approaching it in a nonjudgmental way so they can truly understand the issues.

But, most of all, it's about being persistent. It is all too easy for the world to give up on these children. Our volunteers don't. They are often the only constant adult presence in these children's lives.

Our organization spans the country with more than 900 local community programs. Most programs are called CASA; others have names such as Guardian ad Litem/GAL, Child Advocates or Voices for Children. What unites us all is the shared goal of helping these abused and neglected children find safe, permanent homes. We want to give them back their childhood and a chance for a future filled with hope.

If you would like more information about our cause and the community program nearest you, please call our national office at (800) 628-3233, or visit our website at www.nationalcasa.org.

Achaessa James once told me that, as a CASA volunteer, "You start out to change a child's life and find you've also changed your own." By becoming a CASA volunteer, I promise you that your life and the lives of the children you help will never be the same.

Michael Piraino
CEO
National CASA Association

Poem by Nicole, age 10,
who resides in family foster care.

How can I say thank you to you,
my friend?

When I needed someone to talk to,
you were there.

At times, when I wanted to give up,
you helped me on my way.

How can I just say two words to you,
When I want to give you so much more.

Your heart is made of gold,
But I would not dare spend it, or use it,
I need to know, what can I do
to say thank you?

Should I buy you a diamond ring?

Or a chain made of gold?

No, you see I should not.

For these things anyone can buy.

So as I sit here and think,
I know one thing I can give,
I can give you a friend,
a friend in me.

Acknowledgments

The Child Welfare League of America and the National Court Appointed Special Advocate Association would like to gratefully acknowledge the following children and youth, with their agencies, for the artwork appearing in this book.

Pg 5   Russel L./Shelby B., 12, Colorado Christian Home Tennyson Center for Children and Families: Denver, CO.

Pg 11   Lakerisha B., 12, Colorado Christian Home Tennyson Center for Children and Families: Denver, CO.

Pg 19   Tobias P., 13, Kemmerer Village: Assumption, IL.

Pg 27   Holly H., 16, Hathaway Children & Family Services: Sylmar, CA.

Pg 33   Witney S., 9, Hawaii Department of Human Services: Honolulu, HI

Pg 39   Alisha, 11, McQuade Children's Services: New Windsor, NY.

Pg 45   Christopher, 10, CASA Project of Jackson County: Kansas City, MO.

Pg 51   Charles H., 14, The Children's Campus, Mishawaka, IN.

Pg 57   Cody, 14, Bremwood Lutheran Children's Home: Waverly, IA.

Pg 63   Bobbi, 11, Mount St. Vincent Home: Denver, CO.

Pg 73   Julia H., 16, Connecticut Department of Children & Families: Hartford, CT.

Pg 77   Tommy G., 8, Colorado Christian Home Tennyson Center for Children and Families: Denver, CO.

Pg 87   Wendell L., 18, New York Foundling Hospital: New York, NY.